IN HIS HANDS

Jason C. Webb

WESTBOW
P R E S S
A DIVISION OF THOMAS NELSON

WestBow Press books may be ordered through booksellers or by contacting:

WestBow Press
A Division of Thomas Nelson
1663 Liberty Drive
Bloomington, IN 47403
www.westbowpress.com
1-(866) 928-1240

ISBN: 978-1-4497-5055-8 (sc)
ISBN: 978-1-4497-5054-1 (hc)
ISBN: 978-1-4497-5056-5 (e)

Library of Congress Control Number: 2012907929

Printed in the United States of America

WestBow Press rev. date: 06/27/2012

Foreword

BEING MARRIED TO JASON IS a wonderful, busy, fun, exciting, enchanting, and eventful journey. There are beautiful moments spent with our family and times spent in amazement of everything God has done in our lives, and I cherish each one of these moments. There have been several times when I wasn't sure if I would get to see more of them.

Over the years, there have been times when God was all I could hold on to. He alone was the source of my strength to carry on with my life while my husband was enduring the trials he faced.

There was the bout with cancer, the plant explosion, the poisonous spider bite and ensuing blood infection, and the accident on the interstate right before our anniversary. Throughout all these experiences, I continued to search for God in every way possible. There were times when I thought that my chances to make memories with my husband were over, times of concentrated prayer, and times of being lost. There were heartrending moments when I felt that my heart and everything else in me was being mercilessly ripped out of my body.

When Jason and I first found out about the cancer, I was afraid of being left alone with our infant son and later, during the treatment phase, I became afraid of not being able to have any more children with him. My security and reassurance came through Ps. 91:1–2, verses that to this day reinforce where the strength and refuge for our family is found. The time spent in prayer and communication with God reassured me that everything was in His control. Knowing that kept me at peace.

When the plant Jason worked at exploded, I was at work at a pediatrician's office. The power to the building went out, and all we heard was that something had exploded. I walked outside with a few of the ladies I worked with, and as soon as we noticed the cloud of dark, black smoke, one of the other ladies at the front desk came to the door yelling my name. I turned just as she told me that Jason was on the phone, and it was his plant that had exploded.

As my world crumbled for the second time in less than a year, I felt God's reassurance begin to surround me again. God had softened the pain of this event by allowing Jason to be in good enough condition to call me so I knew he was still alive. As I returned to my desk, I began to shake uncontrollably, immersing myself in prayer to fight off the worries that began to cloud my mind. When I first arrived at the hospital and saw Jason in the emergency room, everything in the room finally stopped spinning and began to clear up. The walls and floor stopped their constant weaving, and began having less resemblance to a desert mirage. When I was able to lay eyes on my husband, all I could say was "Thank you, Jesus."

That was a phrase that would become status quo for me over the next few years through the time of job loss, frustrations of the kids needing their father at home, and more. Prayer had, and still has, the greatest impact on my life to see me through the harsh difficulties, and I have been able to draw closer to God through the tests and trials we have endured as a family. My husband and I found our refuge, strength, and bond with each other was made stronger when we took shelter in the hand of God.

Angie Webb

Welcome to my story.

In attempting to write a book about all God has accomplished in my life, I fear that I have undertaken a daunting, if not impossible, task. I liken it to counting the stars in the night sky or the grains of sand on the beach, as His blessings, gifts, and encounters of endless mercies have been more than I can fathom.

This is my story. I hope you can find solace, comfort, reassurance, and maybe even strength in parts of it to help you resist the temptation of living without experiencing everything God has to offer you. Open your eyes by opening your heart and listening to what God is asking you, asking of you, and whispering in your ear. In 1st Kings 19:11-13, Elijah has an opportunity to meet with God on the top of Mount Horeb. Through a great wind, massive earthquake, an intense fire, and sheer silence, God moved and Elijah was able to experience God firsthand. When your Elijah moment arrives and you are standing on your Mount Horeb, don't miss the moment when God moves in your life.

Thank you for becoming part of my testimony, and may God bless you and yours.

Jason C. Webb

I

 ## In The Beginning

1

In The Beginning

OPEN YOUR MIND'S EYE FOR a moment. Imagine a picturesque summer's day with a beautiful blue sky, fluffy white clouds, and a gentle breeze that perfectly kisses and caresses the side of your face. After a sweat-soaked ride that covered five-plus miles through the neighborhood on a red bicycle with worn-out tires, a voice in the back of your head whispers, "One day, you will work for me. One day, you will preach my word."

For a few brief moments, time seems to stand still. The birds' song seems to dim, the sun shines brighter, and the breeze pauses in mid-flight, suspended by the fact that those words had been spoken.

That was the first time I heard God's voice in such an amazingly audible way that it was undeniable. Everything paused, time stood still as if it was afraid to ruin a moment ordained by the Creator, the Father of all. It seemed that nothing dared to break the silent reverence of the experience. Yet, at the time, I didn't recognize the awesome power in those words. I was destined to be a prodigal son. I would allow myself to wander, lost to those words for years, before returning to embrace them and fully experience everything God had planned for me.

The strange aura of the moment was broken by my stubborn indifference and desire to get to the hose in the backyard for a drink to quench my thirst. The water consumed that day only sufficed for the moment; it wasn't until many years later that I discovered the water of life, the truth that is Jesus Christ.

In a fashion not unlike Abraham's reaction to God's promise of a son (Gen. 17:17), my reaction to those words that day was one of wonder and laughter mired in a nonchalant attitude. I packed those words away in my mind for use at a later time, not really sure if I would ever pay any attention to them. Little did I realize the true impact those words would have in my life.

Gen. 17:17 describes Abraham's reaction to God telling him about a blessing coming in his life: Isaac, Abraham's son. After God had spoken the words revealing the coming birth of Abraham's son, scripture says Abraham laughed. How often do we laugh at what God tells us? Do we see part of ourselves revealed in that passage? So many times we miss the point of the conversation that God is trying to have with us simply because we don't listen with our heart. Just because we hear with our ears doesn't mean we grasp and comprehend the truth of God's words.

God is both direct and indirect in His communication with us. In this passage of scripture, He is direct in His statement to Abraham that he would be blessed with a child and told him, "But My covenant I will establish with Isaac, whom Sarah will bear to you by this time next year" (Gen. 17:21 NIV). However, is God always that direct or clear when speaking to us? Sometimes. Those moments when you know you are experiencing God but are not quite sure of the magnitude of everything are when the beauty of blind faith becomes revealed!

In a time when it was commonplace to run with scissors, drink from the garden hose, stay outside all day long (in some instances to prevent having to come inside and do chores), and other activities that aren't considered safe now, I didn't think about how many "dangers" I was avoiding. The things that didn't kill me made me stronger. Now I realize that God's big arms of love blocked the things that didn't kill me.

I saw a cartoonist's rendition of this scenario one day represented by a man walking along complaining about the small rocks that were hitting him. The next picture displayed Jesus standing there with His arms spread wide with a multitude of rocks hitting Him and being stopped before they ever got to the guy walking.

Oftentimes, we find ourselves in this situation without realizing just how much the grace and mercy of God prevents us from having to deal with. Wow, isn't grace wonderful? The all-surpassing grace of God envelops us like our favorite blanket and snuggles up with us, giving us the comfort that we love to feel.

During my formative childhood years, I was repeatedly like the prodigal son, spending periods of time involved at church and then straying away from it before returning again. Church was like an amusement park ride—a process of getting onto the ride, having the highs and lows, and the ride coming to an end. It was a ride that neither bored me to tears nor secured my interest enough to continue participating.

My childhood church was very traditional. Most members were families who were financially affluent compared with my family, so my brother and I were often looked down on by the other youth. We managed to become the topic of conversation at most of the youth meetings, albeit not in the preferred manner. The majority of the meetings weren't complete without the verbal destruction of the Webb boys—not exactly the optimal situation for an adolescent male who had just had God whisper in his ear.

The few youth trips we endured were filled with verbal attacks, and the ridicule we faced was simply too much for my brother and me to overcome. Obviously, our experiences on those trips are not ones my brother and I look back on with pleasure. We were told we lacked a focus on God and where we needed to be in our spiritual walk. Honestly, my focus at that time was on most anything but God. As a thirteen-year-old boy, girls, games, and sports were my focus.

Growing up in a split-parent home proved to be an interesting situation. My younger brother, mother, maternal grandparents, and I comprised my immediate family. We had a great home life, but church was not a place in which we thrived. At times, it was almost like punishment. My brother and I dreaded hearing the words "Boys, stop playing around. It's time to go to youth group" come out of our mother's mouth.

Our mother and grandparents were sticklers for prayer, and we would be put to bed while learning the Lord's Prayer (Matt. 6:9–13), hymns, and other liturgical writings. Some of my favorite memories to this day consist of the hymns my grandmother would sing to put me to sleep, most notably "Twilight Is Stealing," which I now sing to my children.

The mornings were a mad dash to get everything together for school, and the after-school hours until dinner were full of more of the same. Dinner always began with a prayer, most often offered up by my grandfather, and consisted of asking God to bless the meal and bless it to our bodies and us into His service. Once again, God had a subtle way of sneaking in reminders of the words He spoke to me that day after my bike ride. The process repeated itself day after day, week after week, school year after school year until I got to college. At that point, it got worse.

My freshman year was a blur of alcohol, skipped classes, road trips with guys from school, and eventually withdrawing from college and returning home. I had successfully managed to drive myself into the first lowest point of my life from which I found no recourse.

I spent the next ten months working third shift in a fabric mill, an utterly horrible experience that convinced me I needed to return to school to finish my degree. The work, coupled with the fact that a simply beautiful person came into my life, was plenty of motivation to finish what I had started the previous year. On July 28, 1995, God introduced me to Angela McCall.

The evening I met Angie started out as many others had with an evening trip to a local hot spot with a close friend. I remember the events of that night as if they happened yesterday.

As I walked into a music store, I stopped dead in my tracks after seeing a beautiful young lady on the opposite side. It was one of those "movie moments"—you know, where the camera zooms in on the two young lovers, the background blurs as everything moves in slow motion, and you can tell the only thing they are focused on is each other. She was a little over five feet tall with long, brown, wavy hair and athletic with a beautifully tanned body.

As I walked around the store, pretending to look for certain albums, I noticed the beauty that had captured my attention would invariably appear just a few aisles away from me. The game of cat and mouse had begun, and I was a willing contestant. Before the night was over, God had orchestrated one of the single greatest achievements of my life: I had her phone number. As soon as my friend and I left the store, I looked him in the eye and said, "One day, I will marry that girl."

The first weekend we were together consisted of a dinner date, a trip to meet all the parents, the loss of my high school class ring to her right hand, and church on Sunday morning. On Friday before our date, I spent hours doing what any guy wanting to impress his date does: I cleaned everything possible about my car and myself. I was going to do everything possible to impress this young lady so I could get a second date with her.

I had the evening planned out: I would present her with flowers before taking her to a candlelight dinner at a steakhouse in Boone, North Carolina, followed by a trip to a mountaintop to watch the sunset before taking her home.

After cleaning my Thunderbird at least twice, I got dressed, told my family I would be home late, and headed out to pick up the girl of my dreams. Nervousness and impatience were the highlights of the short seven-mile drive from my house to hers, and both of my "traveling companions" did nothing to boost my confidence. As I approached the turn-in for the road she lived on, I thought, "What's the worst that can possibly happen?"

The "worst" that happened was a phenomenal night. The dinner conversation included pointless topics, as neither of us could focus on anything but each other. The sunset from the mountaintop was picturesque, the sky appearing alive with streaks of color. And the view through the sunroof on the drive down the mountain revealed a perfectly illuminated starry map stretched out on a black canvas, serving as a road map to lead our dreams of what could be into the future.

The wind that coursed through the car blew Angie's hair in every direction, framing her face and highlighting her beauty, which could be found only in the finest Renoir and Van Gogh paintings, while the starlight made her eyes glisten and seep into my heart, taking a portion of it prisoner.

There I was, consumed by an ever-growing interest in this young lady who had just begun her conquest of my heart and finding myself wondering if this night was really happening.

Upon returning to Angie's house, the moments we held onto each other seemed like eternity, and we longed for more. The end of our first date approached with the speed of an avalanche, sweeping us into a current of love that was unlike anything we had ever experienced.

The guy who had been run out of the youth group at his home church because he failed to fit in financially with the others learned about worship with the special someone he had met just two days prior. The church service I attended with Angie that Sunday morning was unlike any I had been to before. Growing up in a traditional, liturgical church, I was unaccustomed to seeing members of the congregation offer up praise vocally apart from the choir or instrumentally as a solo worship offering. It was refreshing and an interesting point God used to draw my attention back to His house.

After lunch that day, Angie and I spent the afternoon sitting together on the couch at my mother's house, learning what we had in common (and what we didn't). We discussed "life, liberty, and the pursuit of happiness"— basically anything we could think to talk about.

We discovered that we both had endured … er, enjoyed … having my mother for a teacher: me for life lessons and Angie for seventh-grade social studies and language arts. We both enjoyed basketball and football; I had played basketball and she was a cheerleader. She had been active in her church and its youth group over the years and insisted that I begin going to church with her for the activities. Somewhere between the big brown eyes that had melted my heart, the sweet voice that pleaded her case, and the intensity of the statement that we would not survive the rest of the year if we weren't in church, I lost the battle, and my defenses about church crumbled. Leave it to God to find yet another way to keep me in His fold when I had decided I would politely excuse myself regardless of whether He or anyone else liked it.

After that first weekend together, Angie and I were inseparable. Always together, always on the phone before and after school, work, and play, people began to understand that if you wanted one of us you got both. Three college degrees and five years later, we were walking down the aisle of the church that had offered us our first worship service together. On September 30, 2000, God allowed me to take Angela McCall as my wife, Angela Webb. God has blessed our journey through good times and bad, for richer and poorer, in sickness and in health.

2

Psalm 91

Ps. 91:1–2 says, "He who dwells in the shelter of the Most High will rest in the shadow of the Almighty. I will say of the Lord, 'He is my refuge and my fortress, my God in whom I trust'" (NIV). God is our refuge, the source of our strength, our very existence. He alone is the reason we are who we are. As trouble rears its ugly head and attacks and challenges us to our core, we are faced with deciding whether to run and hide, face the problem on our own, or run to God and let Him handle it.

When we are challenged, we find out where our focus in life is by the way we handle the situation. How many times have you been faced with a difficult situation, confronted it head-on with a self-righteous attitude while relying on your own abilities, only to fall short of the resolution you needed? Oftentimes, when we place our burdens on our own shoulders, attempting to conquer the situation with our own strength, we don't realize just how much we really compound the problem. I think about the guy who attempts to work on his car at home even though he doesn't know the first thing about car repair. He sets the jack in the appropriate place, gets the car secured, raises it, and begins to work. Even though he knows how to approach the problem, he doesn't have the appropriate knowledge to make the repairs correctly, and the problem always gets worse before it gets better. After many hours of skinned knuckles, dropped tools, misplaced parts, and distractions, he finally gives up and decides to let a mechanic make the repairs.

Don't we attack our problems in the same way? Isn't it our nature (especially us guys!) to fix it ourselves? We are problem solvers by nature. We spend our childhood going to school to learn how to work things out, solve problems, and fix and repair things, but we miss out on Psalm 91. We work hours upon hours, stressing over trivial things, and fail to realize that we don't find our rest in the shadow of God. Jesus said, "Come to me, all you who are weary and burdened, and I will give you rest. Take my yoke upon you and learn from me, for I am gentle and humble in heart, and you will find rest for your souls. For my yoke is easy and my burden is light" (Matt. 11:28–30 NIV). The invitation is there for you to experience rest in Him.

The next time you face a problem that seems overwhelming, why not take it to the professional? Instead of scraping knuckles, losing parts and time, and suffering through life's distractions and interruptions while stressing over something you can't control, give it to God! Find solace in His presence. Allow Him to comfort you, take control of the situation, and make the necessary repairs. After all, doesn't it make sense that God, who created the universe and everything in it, should have no problem at all dealing with your cares and concerns? He already knows about them, so why not talk with Him about them? Matt. 10:30 tells us, "And even the very hairs of your head are all numbered" (NIV). If God knows exactly how many hairs are on your head, He knows what your concerns and problems are.

During the years I taught high school Sunday school classes, I often placed a shoebox at the front of the classroom. I wrapped it as neatly as possible in white paper and drew a cross on the lid. In the middle of the cross, I cut a slot so papers could be dropped into the box. I labeled it as the SFJTD box, or "Something for Jesus to Do" box. The students would take time at the beginning of each class to think about a prayer concern they had, write it down, and deposit it into the box. The purpose of the box was to signify giving the concern over to God, putting Psalm 91 into practice.

Once a month, the students and I would empty the box's contents onto the table and share some of the prayer requests. The youth were astonished at how many of their prayer concerns had been answered. They were able to live out Psalm 91 and reflect on how God had moved in that area of their life.

I continued this practice year after year, and the new students coming into the class would always start off asking about the box. Before long, the box was removed and in its place we put an empty water jug, which quickly filled as well. The visualization of giving things over to God not only impacted the youth but me as well. God had been orchestrating a master plan in my life, developing in me a dependency on Him to handle my problems. I mean, if I didn't practice what I was preaching and teaching, what kind of youth leader would I have been? God made sure I knew what I was talking about.

Isn't it amazing how God chooses to reveal characteristics of His personality? The Bible tells us many things about God, for example, His likes and dislikes, temperament, patience and impatience. We can't understand the depth of God's divine wisdom and unending love until we begin to experience Him in every way possible. We often seek God during times of trials and tests and allow ourselves to skate by during the easier times.

James 1:2–4 tells us, "Count it all joy, my brothers, when you meet trials of various kinds, for you know that the testing of your faith produces steadfastness. And let steadfastness have its full effect, that you may be perfect and complete, lacking in nothing. (NIV)" This verse has meant many different things to me over the years, but I finally understand its impact on my life. For me, it was a combination of simultaneously pushing myself to earn my bachelor's degree, working 50 hours a week, preparing for a new life with my wife, and serving at church.

But shortly after Angie and I engaged, the company I worked for was bought out and closed. Strike one. The following year, when Angie and I got married, the company I worked for sent my department overseas, and once again I was unemployed. Strike two. Next came an employment stint with a computer networking company, which abruptly shut down. Strike three. That should have been it, right? I mean, it works in baseball, why not the job field, right?

Wrong.

The next company reduced its workforce by half two months after I began work. Being the last salaried manager hired, I was the first salaried manager out the door. The same thing happened nine months later at the next company, but this time it happened with a twist. The last layoff occurred right after Angie and I had decided to start a family because my job situation and our finances had stabilized. But in March 2003, a massive layoff eliminated almost one hundred jobs at the plant, including my position, leaving me grasping at straws and searching for direction.

God, enter stage right. Two weeks after learning I was losing my job, I discovered the next great blessing and achievement of my life was on its way: Angie and I were going to become parents.

Those of you who are parents know the feeling of excitement that envelops you when you hear the words, "We're going to be parents." It is one of those moments where you can remember exactly where you were and what you were doing—literally a moment you will never forget. I was standing in the extra bedroom in our first house when my wife called with the news. She was so excited, she couldn't keep the secret until she got home from work. The words "You're going to be a daddy" remain in my head to this day. Immediately, I fell to my knees in a prayer of thanksgiving, seeking God and asking Him to guide me in my new role as a father.

The questions that run through your head after finding out you are becoming a parent are endless—and that is when everything is going well. Finding out a child is on the way when you are unemployed opens the door for the questions to be compounded by worry, multiplied by dismay, and added to uncertainty. It all equals one very troubling mess. Once again, God demonstrated that He alone was greater than all the negatives Angie and I were facing.

The nine months between the phone call that changed my life and the birth of my son, Connor Andrew Webb, flew by. They were spent drawing unemployment checks as my job searches turned up empty. I did handyman work for cash to supplement my unemployment benefits, prepared our house for the new arrival, and prayed.

During this time, I was going through phase one of learning to totally depend on God. He would reveal His presence to me at the most opportune times, showing His grace and mercy in ways that could only be explained as "That's just God working." Every time a bill was paid when we seemed to have no money, that was God working. Every time a need was met, that was God working. Every time we were blessed with a new piece of furniture for the baby's room, that was God showing off.

Two new phrases made their way into my life and the Sunday school classes I was teaching: Pray Without Ceasing and Constant State of Prayer. Pray Without Ceasing, which I shortened to PWC, was a reminder of what scripture tells us to do, and it became the basis for my life. Constant State of Prayer, or CSOP, reminded me to be in constant communication with God.

As God continued to reveal himself through His actions, I began to understand PWC and CSOP. They are a constant mindset, a continual offering of yourself and all you say, think, and do. It requires you to analyze your thoughts, words, and deeds on a deeper level than you have before, while building your dependence and reliance on God. Matt. 19:26 tells us, "Jesus looked at them and said, 'With man this is impossible, but with God all things are possible.'" (NIV).

"With man this is impossible, but with God all things are possible": that was the only possible explanation for why we were still able to prepare for Connor's birth.

The book of Ecclesiastes tells us that all things are for a season. The time of being unemployed came to an end two weeks before Connor was born. Angie and I had learned to become more dependent on God. We had learned how to trust Him more, listen better, and pray harder. We had discovered part of the truth in James 1:2 and learned how to experience joy in Christ even during the most difficult time of our married life to that point. The bills had been met even with little income from me. The nursery was prepped and ready, clothes were in their place, and toys, books, food, and milk were available. God had not simply met our needs; He had exceeded our dreams and expectations.

The job I took just before Connor's birth was as a warehouse manager at a chemical plant. Interestingly, I had no experience in this field. I immediately accepted the opportunity, though, despite the salary was significantly less than what I had made before.

A child's birth is one of the greatest miracles we can experience. It proves the existence of a sovereign God, one who truly loves us and wants us to enjoy life the way He intended it.

The first time I held my son, I was entranced by the warmth of his face, the way he seemed to relax when he heard my and Angie's voices, and the comfort of knowing he was with family. I remember wondering in awe if that is how God looks at us every day. Again, the enormous gift of Jesus, the Son of God, as a sacrifice for each of us was impressed on me. Looking at my son, I simply could not grasp the pain God must have felt when He offered Jesus as the sacrificial lamb.

The first year and a half of my new job passed by without incident. Once again, God had established me on solid ground, and I grew comfortable.

But comfort lasts only so long.

II

 ## Cancer

3

Sick

WHAT DOES IT MEAN TO be sick? Is it simply a head cold with a runny nose and sore throat? Maybe a fever? The flu? How about pneumonia? Sick to your stomach? Does it require a hospital stay? A visit to a doctor? Can staying at home and resting heal your infirmity?

Luke 5:31 says "Jesus answered them, 'It is not the healthy who need a doctor, but the sick.'" (NIV). Does this statement by the Son of God mean that sickness is physical and a doctor must see anyone who is sick? What kind of sicknesses have you dealt with in your past? Physical? Emotional? Mental?

In February 2005, my wife and I noticed a difference in my left testicle: It had become rock hard, definitely abnormal. I called my family doctor and went to the office to be checked. After learning I had not suffered any injuries to my left testicle, the doctor scheduled an ultrasound for the next day.

At this point, the what-ifs began tormenting me. Anyone who has ever been besieged by what-ifs knows they are terrible monsters created for the sole purpose of tormenting any sane individual to the point of questioning anything and everything he or she knows.

As I became overwhelmed by the what-ifs, my world became a whirling dervish of uncertainty: What if there is something really bad wrong with me? What if it's cancer? What if I am going to die? I am only 28 years old, isn't that too young to die? I have a son who is only a year and a half old, so I can't die yet. Maybe I have been injured and don't remember it. If it is an injury, why don't I remember it? What if there is something wrong with my mind? Why can't I remember what happened? What in the world is going on?

The only question I did not ask was "God, why are you tormenting me?" That is a question we must not allow ourselves to ask. There is a reason we endure what we do. The saying "That which doesn't kill us makes us stronger" needs to be amended to "That which doesn't kill us makes us stronger in Christ" or "God makes us stronger by allowing us to endure things we don't believe we can see our way through."

The nights after the ultrasound were endless, sleepless hours of torture. The questions seemed to run continuously through my mind like a broken record left to play to an audience of nobody who cared enough to listen. Finally, an eternity of two days later, I had my follow-up appointment with my urologist. The morning of my appointment, Angie awoke to find me pacing the floor in angst. After some friendly bantering when she mentioned that we would need to replace the carpet if I didn't quit pacing the floor, we were ready to leave.

Upon arriving at the urology clinic, I had to complete a questionnaire. At the time, it was more that I could accomplish because I was so nervous. In between intermittent trips to the restroom, I managed to complete the questionnaire and waited impatiently for the nurse to call my name.

At long last, the moment came. My name was called. With the impatience of a child on a shopping spree at the local toy store, I rushed through the doors and immediately realized that I had no clue where the nurse wanted me to go. After going through the rudimentary checks (height, weight, blood pressure, etc.), the door to an exam room was opened and Angie and I walked in.

Once in the room, I was provided a sealed cup, directed to a restroom, and asked to provide a urine sample. While obtaining the sample, I passed a kidney stone, which the nurse brought to us after the lab had obtained the sample. The joy on the nurse's face as she walked into the exam room and explained "I know why you were experiencing pain now" quickly faded as I informed her that pain wasn't the reason I was being seen. Her response—"Oh, you must be that one then"—did nothing to inspire confidence in me.

As the nurse left the room, the impact of what she said hit both Angie and me with the force of two old steam engines battling for the same section of railroad track. All the breathable air was immediately sucked out of the room as we both sat and waited, fearing the worst possible news.

Two eternities later, Dr. Eller, my urologist, came into the room. After the cursory introductions, he laid down X-ray films and the paperwork containing the results of my blood work on the counter, looked at the two of us, inhaled deeply, and spoke three words that would forever change my life: "You have cancer."

Immediately, I felt my heart stop beating and drop to the floor. I began feeling sick from the top of my head to the bottom of my feet, the room began to spin in circles, and time stopped. Once I regained my normal thought processes, I could hear myself saying to people I would meet in the future, "Hi, I'm Jason. I have cancer. Hope you are having a great day."

Then the absurdity of that introduction hit me. Why was I even thinking about meeting people in the future? I had cancer; I might as well go ahead and pick out a grave marker.

I snapped out of my daydream as Dr. Eller said, "If I had to have cancer, this is the kind I would want. While it is one of the fastest spreading types there are, it is also one of the easiest to cure. If the patient is able to make one year of remission after treatment, the chances of it ever recurring are less than 0.01 percent." Finally, something to hang on to.

Dr. Eller informed us that I would need surgery to remove the tumor. He then excused himself to give us a few minutes to discuss how rapidly we wanted to proceed.

As Dr. Eller walked out of the room and shut the door, Angie and I immediately began to pray. During the next few minutes of prayer, we discovered total dependence on God, part two. We committed my life and treatment into God's hands, agreed that we would follow as He led us, and that no matter what happened, I would end up a winner either way. If God chose to heal me, I would get to enjoy life here with my family and serve God in every way possible. If God chose to bring me home to heaven to live with Him, I would definitely go out as a winner.

Several minutes later, Dr. Eller returned to the exam room to get us. As we followed him down the hallway to a station on the wall where the X-rays could be read, I felt the eyes of the nurses and staff who were familiar with my case watching me. I could almost hear their thoughts—"Dead man walking," "I hate that situation is on that young family," "I wonder if they have any kids he may leave behind."

As we rounded the corner, Dr. Eller placed the scan results on the screen and turned on the backlight. Sure enough, there it was—my tumor. Just mentioning the word "cancer" stirs fear in people's minds, and I had been picked as its next victim. Since cancer appears as white dots on an X-ray, my left testicle looked as though it was playing the role of a snowball in a winter television special.

At this point, the reality of the situation set in, and the steely resolve we all have began to set up residence in my psyche. As my mind and my heart finally got together on the playground of confusion, everything came into focus. I heard God speak once again, "I am not done with you yet. This is part of your testimony. How much do you trust me?" I knew then everything was in His control.

My surgery was scheduled for two days later.

After a day of drudgery, impatiently waiting for the next day to dawn, the morning of the surgery came with new hope shining through the dark cloud of uncertainty surrounding the situation. Many people came to the hospital with me: my wife, my mother, our pastors' wives (one of whom I taught Sunday school with), my best friend Kenneth, and one of my wife's cousins. We all prayed together before the nurse and the anesthesiologist appeared to wheel me to the operating room. I remember the tears streaking down my wife's face, the extreme look of concern shrouding the faces of both my wife and my mother, and the panicked mindset that seemed to ensconce the prayer group that had congregated to see me off on my maiden voyage into the world of cancer treatment. Thank goodness the anesthesiologist gave me the "good juice," as he called it, as my mind registered this panorama of worry. I am not sure I would have been able to allow myself to be wheeled away if I had realized the amount of despair my condition had brought to that group of people.

As I was rolled along the corridor, I was overwhelmed as I thought about the people left behind in the room, how much they cared for me, and the unyielding support they were showing my family. They were people God had placed in our lives specifically to guide us through this moment.

Entering the operating room, I viewed my surroundings through a misty haze that wouldn't dissipate, and as the realization hit that it was from the meds, I whispered a quick prayer for safety and the doctors' ability then passed across the brink that separates the world of the conscious from the netherworld of deep, medicated sleep.

The next thing I remembered was waking up with my throat sore from the breathing tube and asking for ice chips. The nurses were accommodating and soon escorted Angie and my mother back to the recovery room to visit with me. After I was awake and alert, the doctor appeared and said, "The surgery was a success." The cancer had been contained in the left testicle and had not spread into my bloodstream. My lymph nodes checked out normal; a biopsy of the surrounding tissues showed they were normal; and my tumor markers were negative.

Immediately, the world was a better, happier place. The smiles that appeared on everyone's faces reflected the joy found in the promise God had spoken to me. I was reminded that He was orchestrating the testimony and story He wanted my life to carry, and that everything was possible through Him.

I was released from the hospital shortly after the operation but could not work or engage in any activities for a week, most of which was spent in a medically induced state of blissfulness. I remember sitting on the couch, having taken a Vicodin tablet for the pain (per doctor's orders), and feeling as if I was attempting water aerobics while submerged in a jar of Vaseline.

I had been given instructions and the names of doctors to contact for treatment to confirm the cancer was gone. After prayer and recommendations, Angie and I decided to go to Dr. Jones. He practiced at the Cancer Care Center at Valdese General Hospital in a nearby town and had excellent success treating all kinds of cancer. We called the office and set up the consultation for a week after surgery.

The initial phase of my cancer battle had been won through God's blessing of the surgeon's hands, and it was time to look forward to round two.

4

A Promise of Hope

ROUND TWO OF MY CANCER battle began with the consultation with Dr. Jones. After the ten minute drive to the hospital, I was ready to embark on the next leg of the journey. Walking into the Cancer Care Center at Valdese General Hospital was a humbling experience. The patients I encountered were a myriad of people, a melting pot of survivors waiting on their turn to enter remission. I began to wonder if I had to take a number and get in line, as if looking to buy that lucky lottery ticket, or would it simply be sufficient to stand around and wait on a handout?

I noticed the lobby was full of smiling faces and began to wonder if those smiles were forced or honest expressions of joy. People appeared in the space behind the double doors leading to the treatment area, and they were laughing. At this point, I knew everyone on the other side of those doors had lost their mind. They weren't just cancer patients; they were lunatics incessantly laughing at nothing. Maybe that was an effect of the treatment.

Finally succumbing to the notion that everyone who was not part of the medical staff had decided they would be best served by spending the remainder of their days laughing themselves into a mindless oblivion, I decided I would soon join their parade of insanity and enjoy every minute of it.

I reluctantly approached the scrub-clad receptionist behind the desk, taking in the sight of the endless amount of paperwork the gatekeeper to my treatment opportunity had on her desk. I was expecting a nanny-type person with a temperamental disposition, wearing glasses entirely too large for her face, to push a three-inch-thick stack of paperwork toward me with the normal speech: "Fill out all the forms, sign here, here, here, and here. Place your insurance cards on the clipboard, sign here, here, here, here, and here. Lastly, I need fingerprints, blood and urine samples, and a copy of your last will and testament. Thanks, and we will be with you shortly."

Our interaction over my paperwork was nothing like I expected. I was met with a caring smile, a "Good to see you here," two pages of paperwork to fill out, and a pleasant request for my insurance information. Step one flew by quickly, leaving me standing in the wake of nonexistent turbulence.

I took the clipboard from the receptionist's outstretched hand and began the trek back across the fifteen feet that separated one side of the waiting room from the other. Sitting down next to Angie, we began to fill out my medical history.

As we worked through the forms, the significance of treatment stage two began to impress itself on us. I was halfway through all that could be done to try to ensure I would be able to enjoy a long life.

Two other couples were in the waiting room filling out paperwork as well. One couple was elderly, and the other was middle aged, revealing that cancer has no qualms about whom it decides to attack. Three different generations sat in a waiting room, sharing the same unspoken what-if questions that Angie and I had worked our way through. With a smile to say "I know what you are going through," we all shared a momentary glance in each other's direction, then returned to the monotony of our paperwork to prevent further discussion of our condition. As the other couples were called to the back, Angie and I were left to ponder the possibilities that were waiting on us on the other side of the doors leading to the treatment area.

Will the treatment work? What if it doesn't work? What if I'm not even a candidate for treatment? Even though the surgeon said he removed all the cancer cells and saw no sign of them having spread, what if the cancer had already come back, this time with a vengeance?

I had to make myself stop repeating these questions inside my head as the sound of a woman's voice calling my name brought me back to reality. My moment had arrived; it was time to see the doctor. As I stood up, I had to balance myself, check myself mentally, and prepare myself for whatever waited for me on the other side of the doors.

But there was no way to be prepared for what I was about to encounter.

As I walked into the treatment area, the room began to spin. I felt lightheaded and dizzy and had to grab onto Angie for support. Was this part of the sickness? Was this yet another dirty trick that cancer had up its sleeve, to incapacitate me right before I met my oncologist?

I was led to a small room to wait for the nurse. It was a cubby-sized room about eight feet square with barely enough room for a coffee table, three magazines, and four chairs. After sitting in a chair closest to the water fountain, I picked up the Bible on top of the magazines on the coffee table. Randomly opening it, I found myself reading Jer. 29:11-13. Here again was another reminder of God's divine intervention and providence, as there is simply no way I could have ever intentionally opened the Bible directly to that scripture: "For I know the plans I have for you", declares the Lord, "plans to prosper you and not to harm you, plans to give you hope and a future. Then you will call upon me and come and pray to me, and I will listen to you. You will seek me and find me when you seek me with all your heart" (NIV).

That specific passage served up a dose of courage, as I knew with everything in me that God was indeed in control of my life. As soon as I finished reading that passage, my treatment nurse, Melissa, showed up. She would become a friend during my treatment who would help encourage me every time I showed up at the office.

Melissa began our time together that afternoon by introducing herself and getting to know a little about Angie and me. She took my vitals, found out what type of cancer I had been diagnosed with, showed me around the office, and assured me that she was available to answer questions, calm fears, and pretty much anything else that had to do with my treatment. It was very comforting to know that one of the people who would be involved with the process of turning me into a TV dinner was actually interested in finding out some information about me other than how much my insurance would cover.

Melissa then led us to another room to meet with Dr. Jones. At first glance, the room reminded me of the interrogation rooms law enforcement officers use to push suspects for information about a crime. Dark gray walls, a single table with a few chairs, and a backlit board used to view X-ray and CT scan results on two walls of the room contributed to the ominous atmosphere. Coupling that with the knowledge that the office was an area where life and death hung thick in the air made for an uncomfortable wait.

As Melissa helped us get seated in the room, she offered drinks and snacks and informed us that Dr. Jones would be with us shortly. A brief time later, he walked into the conference room and our lives.

"Hello, Mr. and Mrs. Webb. I'm Dr. Jones, the oncologist here at Valdese Hospital. I have been looking forward to meeting you."

"Hello, Dr. Jones. I can't honestly say that I have always dreamed of coming to this type of doctor's office, but since I am here, I am glad I am. The alternative just didn't seem right at this time."

"No, but it has a great retirement plan."

"Are you a Christian?"

"Yes, Jason, I am. Most of my staff here is as well."

"Thank God you are my doctor then."

Dr. Jones was a man of an unimposing, short stature but overflowing with excitement, passion, and a heart for Christ. At first glance, it was a shock to see this doctor, barely taller than the lab coat he was wearing and sporting a full brown beard, walk into the room and introduce himself as the person who would be assisting me in my recovery from cancer. He didn't refer to it as my fight with cancer; instead it was my recovery from cancer. It had to be repeated a third time before I fully understood what he was telling me: recovery from cancer. Dr. Jones wasn't presenting it as a possibility or even an option; he was stating it as if it was a foregone conclusion. Once again, the eternal wellspring of hope based on the promise made by God and the scripture passage found in Jer. 29:11–13 began to well up within my very being.

5

Treatment Begins

THAT EXCHANGE WITH DR. JONES was all it took for me to realize that God had me exactly where He wanted me. From that moment on, the consultation went smoothly. God had placed me in a situation where He knew I would be comforted by the fact that even though I was passing through the valley of the shadow of death, I could find comfort because He had given me a guide to reassure me I would come out on the other side.

Dr. Jones informed Angie and me that the cancer appeared to be contained at the tumor site; my follow-up blood work was clear; and it seemed that the only thing left to do was the radiation treatment. He stated that my condition was not bad enough to warrant chemotherapy.

Dr. Jones urged Angie and me to consider cryopreservation if we wanted more children because of the area of my body that would be treated with radiation therapy. Along with information about where we could go for cryopreservation in Charlotte (about an hour away), I was given a list of certain types of soap to use when washing, as my skin would become very dry and I could possibly suffer from severe sunburn-like symptoms as a result of the radiation, and another list of medications for different symptoms such as nausea, diarrhea, depression, and anxiety. By the end of the consultation, I felt like a walking pharmacy. I was sure there was no way the amount of prescription meds I was carrying ownership papers for could be legal.

The consultation concluded with Dr. Jones, Angie, and me sharing what God had done in each of our lives and saying our good-byes for the time. I was informed that I needed to call back in April to set up a time to begin my treatment regimen.

The following weeks went by in a flash between two trips to the fertility clinic in Charlotte, closing on a new home, and moving. As moving day approached, we were unsure how we would get it all done. I could not do any heavy lifting, but once again, God provided.

The beauty of blind faith is displayed when God shows up and shows off. On the morning of the move, my long-time friend and his wife drove almost two hours to help with the move. And the entire men's Sunday school class from our church appeared with a box truck. All we had to do was tell them where we wanted the furniture and boxes once they were inside the new house. The entire move was done in less than four hours. Isn't it wonderful when God finds willing hearts to help where there is a need?

My first day of treatment arrived. The dawn of that day greeted me with a smile, the warmth of the sun, and a promise of a new future on the morning breeze. Again, the words of Jer. 29:11–13 ran through my mind as if God was sending a simple reminder to keep trusting in His promise that He was, is, and always will be in control.

I went to work that morning, rushed through some paperwork, and headed to Valdese Hospital after lunch to begin my treatment regimen.

Once I arrived, I wondered how many treatments I would have to endure before my inner self created the world of fun and laughter that I had seen others enjoying during my previous visit. After crossing the threshold into the world of treatment, the first person I saw was Melissa. A smile, a notebook, a needle and syringe, and a finger point to a pretreatment room, and we were off into the world of cancer treatments.

I sat in a small chair in the corner of the room, but Melissa informed me that I had the seat of honor in the center. The seat of honor happened to be a chair very similar to the ones used in a dentist's office.

After claiming my temporary perch, I felt as if I should strap in with seatbelts to prepare for the wild ride that was coming my way. The needle and syringe combo presented the possibility of two distinctly different options. The first option was a calming, blissfully unaware state of mind during the impending procedure to ensure I would not remember the process of cooking parts of my body to eliminate the remaining cancer cells. The second option, which was quite less controlling, was just enough to take the edge off, where I would be able to enjoy all the nerve-wracking intensity of the discussion of the treatment preparation and planning.

I soon discovered option two was the planned course of action. As soon as I was as comfortable as possible, Angie latched onto my left hand and found a seat beside me, reassuring me that she would be with me throughout the entire process that day.

One of my biggest fears at the time was the needle. I absolutely hated the thought of any needle stabbing into any part of my body for any reason.

Melissa informed me that we were ready to begin. I closed my eyes in anticipation of the impending pain as the instrument of destruction (the needle) began its deadly assault on my arm. As soon as I had myself geared up for the injection, Melissa calmly said, "Okay, we are done in here, let's move on to the next room."

That was it. The injection was over, and I never noticed a thing. Hopping up from the table, I smiled at Angie and, with her in tow, followed Melissa. We walked past Melissa's desk and entered the holding cell room. Here we were informed that Angie would be able to go into the treatment room for a few moments while they prepped me. Once it was time for my treatment to begin, she would have to leave. Apparently, it is not a good idea for those without cancer to remain in the treatment room during a radiation treatment.

I was handed a towel and a lead sphere that was split in the middle horizontally and informed those two items were all I needed for the treatment periods. At this point, Melissa said good-bye and good luck and told us that the rest of my treatment team would be in momentarily.

Joel was the next nurse I met. He entered the treatment room, introduced himself to Angie and me, and began to put everything in perspective. As he began to outline the treatment process, his ease in speaking to us automatically began to help me relax. I was already somewhat relaxed due to the painless injection of "happy medicine" (as it was called), and Joel's easygoing nature further enhanced my tranquil state.

But as he began to share the secret of the lead sphere, my terror began anew. The lead sphere was a protection unit to help ensure the possibility of me having children in the future. Joel kept insisting proper placement of the top and bottom sections was crucial to my comfort.

After getting as ready as I could make myself, Joel called for the rest of the treatment team to come into the room. There were three more nurses with Dr. Jones who descended on me like vultures on carrion. After circling the table I was laying on, they began their discussion about my case. Then the markers came out—green, purple, and blue magic markers and small hooked needles with capsules containing black ink.

Upon further review of the marking tools, my curiosity grew to grand proportions. They told me the markers were to mark the radiation grid on my torso to assist the staff with properly administering the radiation. What they failed to inform me was the purpose of the hooked needles, though I soon learned.

The hooked needles penetrated the skin and injected something into the body. The needle itself varies in design, some being straight, some curved, some large, some small. However, until this point in my life, I had never seen a needle bent ninety degrees with a small plastic capsule containing black ink. This group of needles was created with one "evil" intention: to inflict as much pain and discomfort as possible while forever marking me with the black ink it contained.

After being sufficiently colored by the staff and their magic markers, the final nurse approached me with a grin on his face resembling the excitement of a young child on Christmas morning. I noticed the tray he was carrying contained six hooked needles, and as he moved closer, my tension grew.

The nurse asked me if I had any tattoos, to which I replied, "I do not." Then he said, "Well, you will in a few minutes."

He took each needle and stabbed me while twisting and squeezing them into their proper locations at the end of the colored highway that had been drawn on my body. He was laying out my radiation grid, which served multiple purposes. It set the boundaries for the radiation treatment and would forever mark me as a cancer patient in case I needed another form of medical treatment in the future.

After my time as an art project ended, it was time for the radiation treatment to begin. Everyone was asked to leave the room, but Joel stayed behind to explain what was about to happen: "Jason, here is what the treatments are going to be like. You will lay flat on your back, as you have been doing, and the machine will rotate around you. You will see it over you, be able to see some plates move on the inside, hear some clicks and whirrs, and then hear a buzz. That buzz is the radiation being applied. You won't feel anything. Then the machine will rotate underneath you, and the same process will happen. All you have to do is lay still and let us do the work."

Joel called out a series of numbers; the machine adjusted from movements the team made in the control room; and then Joel exited the room. Once he rounded the corner to leave the room, he called out a final "Good luck" and I was on my own.

At that point, the coolness of the metal table on my back began to become much more noticeable, and the silence of being the only one in the treatment room inched ever closer to being overwhelming. The solitude added to the silent serenity and eerie awkwardness of the moment, and a battle began to rage inside my head and my heart. It was one of the first times since my surgery that I felt completely alone. No one was by my side to hold my hand and offer assurances and comfort—until God stepped in once again.

In the silence, He spoke louder than the deafening quiet that had overtaken the treatment room. He reminded me that He had put Jer. 29:11–13 in my life for a reason, and it was for times like this that He had ordained that scripture. "Plans not to harm you, but to prosper you … to give you hope and a future" echoed in my head as He took it upon Himself to visit with me in the moments before the treatment began. In a flash, God took the fear that had hit me like a heavyweight fighter throwing a punch to my gut and replaced it with the calm of His presence. There, in that moment, my nerves settled, and I was once again resolved to let go and let God work. I had found the peacefulness that comes only when you let God have total control.

I readied myself as I heard Joel's voice over the loudspeaker asking if I was ready for them to begin. As soon as I replied yes, the machine started to adjust, the plates clicked, and then I heard the buzz. It was exactly as I had been told. I didn't feel anything.

The machine then started to rotate underneath me, moving until it was positioned appropriately. The plates clicked, and there was the buzz again. Lying there on the table, I noticed the panel in the ceiling that housed the lights was painted like a clear blue sky with fluffy white clouds, and I remember thinking "I wonder if that is what part of heaven looks like."

After my treatment was completed, Joel walked into the room with Angie just a step behind. "Jason, that's it. That's all there is to it. Nothing really for you to do except lay still and take care of yourself at home. Can you do that?"

"Uh, yeah, I think I can handle that part. But seriously, that's it? That's all there is to it?"

"Yep, that's it. Why? Is there supposed to be more?"

"No, not at all. It's just that I've always heard that treatments were so much more than that."

"I never said this would be easy or hard either way. With the type of cancer you have, a lot of it is going to come down to what you make out of it. What type of attitude you have, how you take care of yourself—you know, that kind of stuff."

"Well, okay. How many treatments do I have like this?"

"We will let Dr. Jones cover that with you, okay?"

"Sure."

The first meeting with Dr. Jones after that initial treatment was brief and to the point.

"Jason, how do you think the treatment went?"

"Well, Dr. Jones, I made it through it. I think that just about sums it up, doesn't it?"

"Basically, but you have nineteen more to go."

My heart sank to the floor. My treatment plan, we were informed, would consist of five treatments a week, one per day, for four weeks.

"Nineteen more?"

"Yes, nineteen more."

After a long, deep sigh, I said, "Okay, I can make it through."

6

Routine

THE NEXT FOUR WEEKS WERE filled with daily treatments Monday through Friday. My day consisted of waking up nauseated, going to work for the morning, eating a small lunch, and then heading to Valdese Hospital for my treatments in the afternoon.

Each session was similar to the previous one. The conversations between Melissa and me would be routine, filled with humorous references to each part of the trip through treatment. When I was undergoing the actual radiation treatment, I equated myself to a TV dinner in the microwave. The small room where I had to wait before each trip had morphed into the holding cell.

"Hey, Melissa, I'm here to be microwaved!"

"Hey, Jason, we are ready for you. Head back to the holding cell."

"I'm on my way there now. See you in a few."

Joel would appear moments after I sat down, often when I began reading a chapter in the Bible. I would spend my few moments in the holding cell browsing through random chapters in the Bible, searching for a piece of God's word that would serve up a dish of comfort for me to carry into the treatment room.

"Hey, buddy, are you ready for it today?"

"Yeah, let's get it. I've got to get to a seven-course meal at a buffet as soon as I leave here, so I don't have lots of time to waste" became my standard reply to Joel's daily question, even though we both knew there was no way I was heading out for that amount of food after the treatment.

Almost two weeks into my treatment regimen, the nausea hit. Some days it would rack my body for hours, leaving me helpless to do anything but remain motionless in bed, moving only to make a mad dash to the bathroom when it crossed the line between manageable and overwhelming.

At some point between the middle of the second week of treatment and the beginning of the third week, the kidney stones began their relentless assault on my body. Between the nausea and the pain from the kidney stones, I had basically moved into my bathroom. The days when I wasn't confined to the bathroom were spent going to work and trying to retain a semblance of a normal life.

By this point, I also began to understand why the staff at Dr. Jones' office had recommended using soap with moisturizing lotion when I bathed. My midsection had begun to develop a severe burn from the radiation. My daily routine grew to include coating the treatment area with aloe and lotion to ease the pain and help the burn heal. I lost hair only in the area treated with the radiation.

Slowly, the second week turned into the third, during which more of the same experiences occurred. With each passing treatment, my body tried to rebel more and more, reaching out to me as if to say that it had endured enough. My body was tired. I was exhausted mentally and physically.

Painstakingly slow, the third week of treatment crawled along until I was in the fourth week. At this point, I realized this chapter in my cancer battle was coming to an end. One more week to go and the light at the end of the tunnel had begun to shine a little brighter. With each passing day, that light kept getting brighter and brighter, its glow intensifying with each treatment I completed. Even though the burns, hair loss, nausea, and kidney stones remained my constant companions, the knowledge that I was about to cross the finish line encouraged me to persevere. I knew God had truly guided me through the valley of the shadow of death (Psalm 23), and the road to exit the valley wasn't much longer.

Finally, the last day of treatment arrived. It appeared at my front door as a visitor who you knew was on its way; you just weren't fully prepared for the visit. After knocking on the door, it politely deposited its baggage and left. It was a blink-twice-and-it's-gone experience. The only remnants of its visit were questions that waged an internal battle between my heart and my head.

With the treatments over, I was on my own. They were no longer the security blanket to help me stay confident that the cancer was gone. I had to rely on blind faith from that point. Much as the lepers whom Jesus healed (Luke 17:11–19), I had to remind myself daily that Jesus had healed me from the disease and to make sure I was the one who said, "Thank you, Lord!" Even in the times of doubt, I would turn to this scripture to remind me that He had endured everything I had and by His grace I had been brought through the fire. I had come out victorious, riding on the coattails of the Creator of the universe. Jesus had truly been my saving grace.

The months following the end of my treatment contained routine activities: work, church, rest, play. I had a new lease on life. I would receive my reminder phone calls about coming in for my follow-up scans to make sure the cancer hadn't spread. Every time I got ready to open the door to the doctor's office or the hospital, anxiety and worry tried to serve as my bellhop. It was up to me to suppress those feelings. Again, I had to remind myself to focus on the promise God had given me that first day I spent in the oncology center at Valdese Hospital - Jer. 29:11–13. Once I was able to place my focus on those verses, my smile returned, and I would breeze through my checkups.

My final visit with Dr. Jones was on January 26, 2006. Almost a year had gone by since my cancer diagnosis. Dr. Jones met me in the room we had used for my consultation, carrying my latest set of scans. After shaking hands, we each took a seat.

"Let me show you what we are seeing on this last set of scans you had done, Jason."

"Okay, but we are good as long as we don't see snow, right?"

"Exactly. As you can see, there is nothing there. Absolutely nothing. Perfectly clear. God has worked a miracle on you. No denying that."

Immediately, my heart started rejoicing. But Dr. Jones wasn't done yet.

"If I didn't know you, know your history, and hadn't seen your surgery scar, I wouldn't be able to tell you had ever been sick. Honestly, the only time I ever want to see you again is if we meet on the street in town. Now that you are basically a year out from treatment and diagnosis, the chances of your cancer returning are less than one half of one percent. In other words, it isn't coming back. And in spite of the percentages, we both know you are healed because He took care of it."

God had delivered me from the lowest point of my life, and I was so much better for it. I had found the meaning of a deeper relationship with Jesus and a deeper resolve inside myself. It was the type of resolve that more often than not is extracted from the innermost parts of a person's psyche due to a catastrophic event in his or her life. I had discovered a new identity—not just who I was but, more importantly, who I needed to be in Christ. But peace on the mountaintop lasts for only so long.

III

BOOM

7

The Day That Changed My Life — Again

WHEN SOMETHING SO PROFOUND HAPPENS that it causes the course of an individual's life to be altered forever, it usually can be attributed to a major event. Marriage, the birth of a child, and the death of a close friend or family member can all be considered life-altering events.

Being involved in any type of stressful situation can have negative or positive effects on a person's psyche. Coming to know Jesus as Lord and Savior is life altering and can bring about beautiful changes in a person's life. The spectrum of the effects of change in someone's life can be as broad and dynamic as a palette of colors on an artist's canvas. It can also invoke a range of emotions that can spread from building something beautiful to destroying everything nearby.

Change can become a catalyst for this range of emotions and can spark an ignition source for the entire spectrum of emotions to be unleashed with the ravaging power of a category five hurricane. Changes that twist your emotions can manipulate you to extremes you never imagined being capable of experiencing. You will see life in the most vivid array of color. The highs and lows will be higher and lower than any you have endured before. Change always seems to hit when it is least expected.

After spending time on the mountaintop, whether it is a few hours, days, weeks, months, or years, complacency sets in. It happens to all of us. For some it happens more quickly, and for others it takes awhile for it to hit, but eventually it gets us all. Just when you settle into the pattern of normalcy, life has a way of reaching out and slapping you in the face.

After hearing the news that my cancer was gone and wasn't going to come back, I was on top of the world. I had a new lease on life and a beautiful family to enjoy.

The weekend following my release from radiation treatments was spent in celebration. Angie and I told everybody the good news. So many phone calls, cards, visits, and more demonstrated how much relief those close to us felt about my release from care. We became inundated with congratulatory well wishers.

Things moved along at a breakneck pace, and my family and I were able to move forward without worry, once again enjoying everything life had to offer. It's unbelievable how quickly things can change.

On January 31, 2006, the day began the same as many other January days in Morganton, North Carolina, had during my previous twenty-nine years. It was a bright and crisp winter morning, sunny with a slight breeze that carried on it the chill of snow from the mountains. Like the previous three mornings between my release from cancer treatment and that day, it held the promise of new, exciting opportunities waiting to be discovered.

After parking my truck in my usual spot at work, I stepped out of the cab, deeply inhaled the fresh air, and spent a moment reflecting on what a beautiful gift God had provided in the dawning of that day. Locking the truck, I headed into the locker room area to punch in and prepare for the workday.

I remember being nonchalant about having to spend more time going through all the tedious files that were under review as the company prepared for audits. Little did I realize that God had given me that task for a reason.

The workday started and progressed normally until the morning production meeting. The first clue that something was amiss should have hit the management team like a two by four in the back of our skulls, but we missed the importance of the news that there was a small problem in the plant.

Ross (vice president), Joan (corporate accountant/human resources), Gary (chemist), Richard (plant superintendant), Christy (purchasing agent) and I sat around the table in the conference room to discuss the activities for the upcoming day. Ross called the meeting to order. We proceeded with the usual conversations, beginning with Richard giving an update on the status of plant activities, and I presented current orders and inventory issues. Gary touched on anything that needed attention from the lab/inspection side, and Joan brought any needed attention to issues from human resources.

Joan and I were in the process of revamping the company's regulations and programs and preparing for several audits, so we addressed those concerns during the meeting. Before we all dispersed, Richard informed us that he had met with Tom, the plant manager, before the meeting. Apparently, there was a "situation in the plant," but Tom had it under control. None of us at the table realized how much this situation would affect our lives.

8

The Calm Before The Storm

As THE WORKDAY WORE ON, I spent my time preparing the company for the upcoming audits, working on organizing files, making sure batch records ("recipes" for our products) were up-to-date, and ensuring our compliance with federal Environmental Protection Agency regulations for hazardous materials. After Joan and I had set up a workstation in the main office trailer, located apart from the main plant, to minimize distractions while preparing for the audits, Joan left for an early lunch. Having been given some unexpected quiet time, I reviewed batch records for accuracy and compliance with what we had quoted to the company's customers. Gary and I reviewed the formulations, other associated paperwork, and one product at a time, putting our stamp of approval on each item.

Joan returned from lunch with her husband around 11:30, and we continued the task of preparing the plant for the audits. But nothing could have ever prepared us for what was about to happen.

If anyone ever tells you that time stands still for no one, don't believe him. While it is true that time doesn't actually stop, a particular moment in time can become permanently burned into your mind and recalled at a moment's notice. The ability to instantly recall a specific moment in your life can produce a rush of sensations that course through you with the force of a tsunami. Your body will react years later in an almost identical way as it did when the original event occurred.

9

Time Stands Still

11:42 a.m.

Time didn't merely stand still; it completely stopped. I looked out the window in Joan's office to check on my shipping dock and see if any drivers were waiting to be loaded. Not seeing anyone there, I returned to my paperwork. But something didn't feel right.

I turned to take another look and will have the next images etched into my mind forever. What I witnessed was beyond comprehension. One minute the plant was there in its decrepit, rundown condition. The next moment there was nothing. Horrified, I watched as the brick and mortar walls of the plant bowed out, tried to collapse inward, and then blew completely apart. The plant rippled as if it was mimicking the surface of a lake on a breezy summer day, teasing the peacefulness only to cast everything into total chaos.

The wall of the plant that had been my shipping dock blew through the parking lot like a runaway train, steamrolling its way across the road fifty yards away. The roof became a ballerina, gracefully pirouetting in midair several hundred feet up before plummeting back onto the remains of the building.

A fireball of monstrous proportions bellowed out of the rear side of the plant, consuming everything in its path as it headed toward the office where I was. After rocking a pickup truck, the fireball dissipated right in front of my eyes, just ten feet from the office window.

Following on the heels of the fireball was the concussion. We have all seen the effects of air moving (i.e., leaves blowing, grass swaying lazily in a breeze), but to see it wrinkle on itself like a blanket and move is a totally different sight. Everything contorted and twisted into grotesque momentary statues resembling gargoyle-inspired architecture from a medieval time period, only to expand and return to a semi-normal state after the air settled back into place. Trees with expansive root systems became projectiles, as if they were fired from a high-caliber gun, flying through the air on a search-and-destroy mission. Fire hydrants became useless as they were blown from their mounts into cars and across the street.

I watched with increasing horror as the concussive wave from the blast continued approaching the office trailer where I was. The trailer where plant employees changed into their uniforms was blown onto its front side only to settle with the back of the double wide completely destroyed.

I threw Joan onto the floor, shoving her under the desk with not a second to spare as the concussion from the blast hit her office. The blast picked me up and blew me through the back wall of her office, my left side hitting the wall squarely. My left ankle hit the edge of her desk, causing it to split horizontally through the middle of the joint. The impact shoved my left shoulder further into the joint than normal, and my left hip was injured as well. I fell beside Joan as part of the ceiling collapsed on us.

11:43 a.m.

I threw off the ceiling, a closet door, and a filing cabinet that had fallen on us so we could escape Joan's office. That's when we saw that the true horror of the situation far exceeded what saw from her office.

All the windows in the office trailer we were in had been shattered by the blast. The front door to the office, which was made of solid oak, had been blown off its hinges and lay in the middle of the trailer, ten feet from where it should have been mounted.

Heidi, who worked in the main section of the office trailer, was a first responder. She met me at the hole in the wall that used to be our front door while Ross appeared in the area that had previously been his office. He looked at me with eyes wide open from fear and uncertainty and asked the question that was on everyone's mind: "What has happened?"

11:44 a.m.

Ross, Gary, Joan, Christy and I staggered out of the office trailer into a world full of madness and sheer chaos. Everyone's vehicle now contained parts of the plant. The building was engulfed in flames with black smoke still billowing up into the mushroom cloud. The powder room, a small structure that was used to shake powder from totes into drums, was demolished. The refrigerated room where we stored our heat-sensitive products no longer existed. The lab, which had undergone massive restoration, looked nothing like it had before the blast. Cardboard drums burned as if they were funeral pyres, while plastic drums melted wherever they lay.

11:45 a.m.

After a quick call to my wife to let her know what had happened and that I was still alive, I began to survey the scene. Hollywood couldn't have created a more intense scene.

The other employees and I could still hear drums exploding inside the plant, generating a cadence for the building's death song. Intermittently, a steel drum would over pressurize and shoot skyward, only to explode like fireworks on the Fourth of July. Slowly, the plant employees began to make their way from the building to the main parking lot. We could hear the sirens wail as emergency personnel made their way to the disaster. As the employees grouped together in the parking lot, I initiated a head count and realized that Bob, our maintenance supervisor, had not emerged from the building.

Joan's husband immediately returned to the plant. He called out to me for help, having found Richard lying outside the entrance to the top floor of the plant. We assessed the situation and decided we needed to move him because a nearby utility pole was on the verge of falling, and the transformer mounted at the top of the pole had begun to arc bright green bolts of electricity.

Richard had sustained a head injury from falling, but we took our chances and decided to move him. As Joan's husband and I carefully moved Richard, Heidi had begun doing what she could with the other employees.

My cell phone had been ringing nonstop since the explosion, and one call I received was from another brother in Christ who was the shift manager at a nearby grocery store. He offered to bring bottled water and whatever first aid items we needed that the store stocked.

The moans of the employees, the screams and shouts of the emergency services crews, the sirens from the rescue vehicles, and the whirr of the news helicopters flying overhead blended together in a raucous symphony.

Finally, the ambulances arrived, and EMS workers began administering first aid to the employees. One by one, those who needed to be were transported to the hospital. I continued to search the wreckage for Bob, frantically pacing the area where we had been confined.

I heard someone call my name and yell for help. My heart began to race as I recognized the voice as Bob's, and my eyes frantically searched the wreckage. As soon as I spotted him, I directed the rescue workers to his location and yelled back that they were on their way. Those words were Bob's last - he died three days later.

Bob and Richard were airlifted to different hospitals equipped to handle their injuries. As soon as they were gone, I returned to the management trailer to begin digging through the paperwork Joan and I had been feverishly trying to organize, looking for a particular folder.

On my way back to Joan's office, I noticed the toilet in the hall bathroom had been transformed into a bidet. The floor had begun flooding from the ruptured water lines, and precious files were being damaged. Joan and I pulled the computers and as many boxes of files as possible out of the office and locked them in my truck. After I made another trip inside the trailer to retrieve more files, I learned that Ross and Joan had finally allowed themselves to be taken to the hospital. I was informed that

Joan had been experiencing chest pains, and Ross was convinced by the paramedics to go to the hospital.

I was hunting for the major from the police force that was in charge of the scene to deliver some requested files when my asthma began acting up. My chest grew tight, making it difficult for me to breathe, and my vision became fuzzy, with a darkness growing in the middle of my field of vision. So one minute I was standing upright carrying files and the next Christy was asking me where my inhalers were while emergency personnel were placing IV lines in my arms and an oxygen mask on my face.

Panic set in at that point. I had been running on pure adrenaline, prioritizing things by need and impact on the situation. But now having been knocked down and basically out by the savageness of the asthma attack in conjunction with the fact that my forehead collided with the hood of a patrol car as I fell, I realized how little I could do at that moment. That realization combined with the fact that the fire had to be getting near the hazardous goods storage area brought on a new sense of urgency. I struggled against the emergency personnel, trying to no avail to remove the oxygen mask from my face and only furthering my weakened state.

Remains of my office

Lab side of the plant

Remains of my warehouse

10

Aftermath

AFTER BEING LOADED IN THE ambulance, the EMT who climbed in the back with me handed me a collection of cell phones and walkie-talkies to assist the communication between me and the major and response teams. I informed the response teams of the danger of letting the fire get too close to the hazmat storage area because more than three hundred fifty-five-gallon drums filled with flammable and corrosive materials were stored there. If the fire got to that storage pad, the entire side of town where the plant was located would light up like Times Square on New Year's Eve.

During the ambulance ride to the hospital, between the phones and walkie-talkies, I tried to inform the firefighters of the types of chemicals in storage. Once the ambulance got to the hospital, the phones were taken away from me, and I was ushered into a trauma room. Once again, there I was in a treatment facility with a team of doctors and nurses descending on me.

While the medical staff surrounded me, I saw my wife's tear-streaked face as my father-in-law, Marshall, and brother-in-law, Andy, peered into my room, trying to get a glance in order to provide some comfort to Angie. As soon as I was informed everything checked out okay and my breathing and heart rate had returned to normal, Angie, Marshall, and Andy walked into my room.

After some idle conversation about how I must have the worst luck in the world, I learned I would not have to stay overnight for observation and would be able to leave shortly. I eased out of bed and painstakingly walked through the emergency department, checking on the rest of the guys from work. After a brief visit with each of them, I was discharged.

The short walk from the emergency department to the car proved to have almost as much excitement as the events of the morning did. The media were not allowed inside the hospital, so my coworkers and I knew the questions we would face when we exited the hospital. Using a police escort to reach our vehicle, we were surrounded by the media. Shoving cameras and microphones in our faces, they hurled questions at my family and me nonstop as we walked to the car, continuing to do so after we were inside the car and had locked the doors. The police continued to run interference between us and the media until we were able to leave.

After leaving the hospital, I immediately called my mother. She was at a friend's house and had her own little support group there with her. I had called her briefly during the chaos at the plant to let her know I was alive but didn't get the opportunity to talk at length with her until we met at her friend's house. It was then that I learned she had been at a gas station a little over a mile down the road from the plant when the explosion occurred. It created such a force, the gas pumps moved at the station where she was fueling her car. When she saw the mushroom cloud, her only thought was that I had been killed and, in driving to the friend's house, she passed by the road that led to the plant.

As I struggled to get out of my wife's car, I began to notice how my body was stiffening up and beginning to ache in ways I never thought possible. My entire spinal column from the base of my skull down to my waist felt as if someone had hot glued a steel beam to my body. The ringing in my ears and the pounding inside my head felt like a construction crew was working there.

Every step I made toward the house was an accomplishment because the pain from my headache continued to intensify, reaching areas of my head that had never experienced pain before. It was a small victory celebrated by the construction workers firing a twenty-one nail gun salute.

Covering the twenty feet between where my wife had parked the car and the front porch of the house where my mother was became the next obstacle I faced after my release from the hospital. I knew if I could walk that distance, it would reassure me I was still capable of functioning.

Walking through the door of the house and seeing my mother standing there with a look of relief, praise, and thanksgiving helped me stand a little straighter. We spent a few moments with her until I began to hurt past the point of putting on a happy face, so my wife and I took our leave and headed to Connor's preschool. I was determined to hold my son.

On our way to the preschool, Angie and I noticed more news vans circling the town looking for survivors and others who had been close by the explosion, each crew looking for that special bit of information the other reporters wouldn't be able to get. We picked up a tail on the way to the preschool that stayed with us halfway through town, eventually deciding that we weren't one of the explosion survivors.

At the preschool, as at all the schools in the surrounding area, everything was locked down. The only way children could leave was if their parents signed them out. Angie went into the school to get Connor, and as I experienced the first few moments of solitude since that morning, the shock really began to settle in.

I found myself staring at the dashboard, the floorboard, my hands, anything to keep from looking out the windows. I was afraid of seeing a news van with a reporter and a cameraman or the fireball that consumed the plant that morning.

Another child's parents pulled into the parking space beside us to pick up their child. As they slammed the car doors, they began muttering something about some stupid person had to blow up a chemical plant that shouldn't have been operating anyway and now their day was ruined. The doors slamming sounded like a drum of chemicals exploding, and I promptly jumped so far out of my skin I could almost see myself sitting next to me. Part of me wanted to run and hide, while another part wanted to scream at the person, "You think your day is bad?" and yet another part wasn't sure what to do.

A few minutes later, Angie and Connor returned to the car, and we headed home. The smile on my son's face, the cheerfulness in his voice when he saw me in the car, was enough to make me grin and warm my heart. I remember looking into his eyes, seeing the joy, and thinking of how I had to be strong for him. The drive home was filled with his questions about why everyone was locked inside the school, why did everyone's parents have to sign them out, and stories from his day.

As soon we walked into our house, chaos resumed. The answering machine was at capacity with messages from family and friends of concern and love, and more from reporters looking for comments and any other information I would share. I was bewildered by the blindingly fast pace in which they were able to find out my contact information and begin their assault on my privacy. Turning on the television was pointless because every channel had coverage of the plant explosion in all its glory. Reminders of what had happened that morning were everywhere, as if any were needed.

My mind was a confused, jumbled mess, but somewhere in the midst of my shattered reality was the voice of God, a whisper that spoke loudly enough to be heard over everything else: "I am here and I love you."

As my mind continued its ballet of torture with the partner fate had cast on it, my body began to pay attention to the damage done to it during the opening act of the day's activities. My back began to tighten up past the point of any possibility of movement. My left ankle started to swell to the point of being almost impossible to put weight on. My left shoulder, which had served as a battering ram against the back wall of the office, was throbbing constantly. I began to think that the construction crew that had set up permanent residence in my head had called in for reinforcements, and the entry point for that second team was my chest and shoulders.

The ringing assaulting my ears had all the forcefulness and power of Beethoven's *Fifth Symphony* being masterfully performed by a royal philharmonic orchestra, while the percussionists pounded out a cadence. While the work in the construction zone reached a fever pitch, I realized it was conveniently located between the two orchestras. The orchestra on the right side would perform a selection from the symphony, and then the counterpart on the left would immediately fire back at a higher intensity and volume. The work crew continued the cadence, keeping time so neither symphonic orchestra would lose their place in the never-ending symphony of agony.

I began to hurt in places I didn't know could hurt. My spirit cried out to God for healing. My body cried out to God and everyone else around for respite from the pain, while my heart cried out for peace. Somewhere in the midst of the torment, I drifted off to sleep.

11

Overload

WORDS MOST COMMONLY ASSOCIATED WITH sleep include comfort, rest, peace, and dreams. Sometimes, words like restless, worried, and anxious creep into the realm of sleep. Not only can sleep be characterized by words but also by actions. People have a tendency to relive certain events while sleeping. When these reenactments occur, they are as real to the person as the event was when it happened. They are commonly referred to as flashbacks.

For the next year, flashbacks became common for me. They began their assault on my sanity the first night after the explosion. As soon as I shut my eyes, I would hear the boom of the primary explosion and sit straight up in the bed in a cold sweat. It would take hours before I could shut my eyes again. The first night, each time I closed my eyes, the scene would automatically restart. I fell asleep out of exhaustion around five the next morning.

By 8:30 a.m., the phone was ringing. It was the vice president of the company requesting I come back to the plant—or what was left of it. He told me that the Environmental Protection Agency, the Occupational Safety and Health Administration, and local law enforcement representatives were requesting (read: politely requiring) my presence at the site.

Barely able to walk, I somehow was able to dress myself and gather the strength to return to the plant. During the drive to the plant, the events of the previous day began an unending video tribute in my mind.

After parking my car, the first thing I noticed was the thick smell of the acrid smoke still hanging in the air.

Making my way through the blast site was a difficult task, made even more so by the images running through my mind of the previous day. I saw the spot where Bob had finally scratched and clawed his way out of the rubble and could see him still standing there calling out to me for help. Smoke still poured out of the building as fires burned and smoldered internally. Almost twenty-four hours later, the site was unchanged from the last time I had been at work.

A question from one of the Chemical Safety Board representatives broke my silent reverie, and as I stared blankly into his eyes, the impact of what I was reliving at the moment hit him. With a pat on my shoulder, he quietly apologized and asked if I could find him in a few minutes after collecting my thoughts. Moments later, wiping tears from my eyes, I turned away from the carnage and prepared myself for the endless barrage of questions that were inevitably going to overload my senses.

Walking into the staging area with the federal agents and disaster control staff was eerily similar to celebrities being engulfed by cameras, microphones, and recorders at a movie premiere. Ten thousand questions attacked my neurological system simultaneously, creating sensory overload, which pushed the limits of my mental capacity and my ability to endure, almost to the point of breaking:

"Where was this chemical stockpiled?"

"Did you really have DMEA (DiMethylEthanolAmine) stored in this area?"

"Where was your silicate storage area?"

"Batch records. I need your batch records. Where in the world are your batch records?"

"Can someone tell me where the methanol, ethanol, and toluene storage area was?"

"How much toluene was supposed to be on hand versus how much actually was physically here?"

"How can you be sure that specific amount of toluene was present in the reactor when it exploded?"

"What is the procedure for ensuring that the manhole on the reactor is securely fastened?"

"Was it SOP (standard operating procedure) to only use four of the retaining bolts to secure the lid on the reactor?"

"Why were the improper chemical amounts used in the mixture in M1 reactor? That was the name of the reactor that blew up, right? Can some of the employees not read the batch records properly?"

Amidst all the questions, the world slowly began to get dark around the edges. When I realized where I was, I found that Joan and I had walked away from the crowd and were standing in the area that afforded the best view of the crews working on the plant. I finally broke the overbearing silence.

"How long do you think it will take for this mess to get cleaned up? Is the owner on his way over from France yet?"

"Jason, I don't know. He should have flown out yesterday, but since I don't have an office anymore, I can't check my voice mail. Do you think this will bother us long, or will we be able to get past it one day?"

"Joan, I'm not sure we will ever get past this."

12

Faith, Grace, and Me

WHEN YOU REALIZE JUST HOW great God is and how uniquely He operates, the power in that realization is overwhelming. As the days wore on, I began realizing once again how much God had intervened and how much I had to be thankful for. I had survived the blast. I watched as a window shattered and shards of glass flew at me, as I was blown through a wall, and had a ceiling fall in on me. Why shouldn't I be thankful?

As I sat and reflected on the window and how the glass flew toward me like a thousand arrows when it shattered, I realized that God had protected me. I was unscathed by the razor-like pieces of glass that had shot around the office like a swarm of mad bees.

Yes, my ears still rang. My vision was still blurry. My body hurt in ways and places I didn't know could hurt. I could barely walk, but somehow I found favor with God. He had brought me through that trial. Much like He had been with Daniel in the lion's den and Shadrach, Meshach, and Abednego in the fiery furnace, He was with me. Psalm 23 took on a new meaning and importance in my life:

The Lord is my shepherd, I shall not be in want. He makes me lie down in green pastures, he leads me beside quiet waters, he restores my soul. He guides me in paths of righteousness for his name's sake. Even though I walk through the valley of the shadow of death, I will fear no evil, For you are with me; your rod and your staff, they comfort me. You prepare a table before me in the presence of mine enemies; You anoint my head with oil; my cup overflows. Surely goodness and love will follow me all the days of my life, and I will dwell in the house of the Lord forever. (NIV)

This passage now holds a greater meaning for me than it ever did before. I know now what it means to have walked through the valley of the shadow of death, and the realization of that began to unfold as I sat outside the fence on the morning of February 1, 2006, and watched the plant continue to smolder. Yes, God had prepared a table before me. Yes, my cup was overflowing with mercy. Yes, my comfort had arrived in the words that He had spoken. Yes, God led me beside still waters and allowed me to find peace in the midst of all the turmoil. Truly, God was greater, and is greater, than all those obstacles facing me.

After enjoying the silence of the moment, Joan and I slowly headed back into the flurry of commotion that was the federal, state, and local governments in action.

In the midst of the constant questioning by the different agencies, my coworkers and I noticed the news crews were beginning to encroach on our encampment. When we were allowed a break from the "inquisition," Joan, Ross, Gary, and I gathered together and began to walk away for some silence.

As we mindlessly strayed from the agents, we began to hear another voice. A reporter from one of the local news stations was preparing a report to air at lunchtime and had reported multiple fatalities from the incident. We collectively blew a gasket. Joan proceeded to the news crew and immediately informed the reporter that she was "very horribly, totally mistaken."

We learned something about newscasts that day. Reporters will tape several different scenarios of an event so they will be the first to have the "latest, greatest version of the breaking news" once the facts have been confirmed.

After Joan paused to take a breath, the reporter and her crew offered their apologies and prayers. Joan apologized for overreacting like she did, and we spent a few minutes answering questions off the record and without any recording devices.

The next two weeks progressed in much the same way, with seemingly endless questioning broken by small respites for lunch and coffee. The weather in the foothills of NC in February sets the perfect stage for needing extreme amounts of coffee, especially when nine hours a day are spent in the blustery cold. So heavy coats, coffee in amounts that were probably against all surgeon generals' health warnings, and frequent trips inside the American Red Cross relief station for warmth and the absence of questions were status quo.

Eventually, the questioning forced me to shut down. My mind and my body began to feel as if they were encased in concrete, and nothing from the outside world was allowed to enter into the sanctuary of solitude I had created for myself.

Three weeks after the explosion, I was released from my obligations to the federal government and allowed to stay home. The opportunity to stay home instead of having to relive daily the cataclysmic events of January 31, 2006, at the plant came as a welcome relief to my body. My mind, however, had ideas of its own.

I couldn't look out of windows, because each time I saw the fireball that charged the office. I couldn't look at a ceiling fan for fear of it falling on me. I became a recluse in my own house.

If you have never lived in fear, it is something that can be conquered only by the grace and power of God. It is something that no other person can describe; only you know the fears you face, the duration of each panic attack, and the things that can cause your fears to surface.

However, God knows your fears. He knows the amount of time you spend suffering, enslaved by the thoughts and emotions that torment you. You only have to trust in Him and allow Him to help you. Malachi 3 talks about God being like a purifier of silver. A person who purifies silver works it over a fire through a very slow process, gradually removing each blemish until nothing is left except the finished product. Allow God this freedom in your life to put you through the fire until all your blemishes are removed.

Right after the explosion, my mind became so engrossed with worrying about whether the building I was in was about to explode, I couldn't spend any time on almost anything else. There was some contact with the company almost weekly, but at the end of March, all the hourly employees were laid off. We got the news at one of our status and update meetings that all benefits would terminate in the middle of April. We would be eligible to draw unemployment and continue with any workers' compensation issues related to the accident. But effective April 14, my coworkers and I would join the ranks of the unemployed.

13

Acceptance

UNEMPLOYED AGAIN. THE ECHOES OF that statement rang endlessly throughout the hallways of emptiness in my mind. Part of me wanted to throw my hands up in despair, almost to say, "What else can happen now?" But that same part of me was afraid to ask this question, not sure if I really wanted to know the answer. Another area of my mind instantly began seeking God, asking Him for wisdom to know what to do and how to handle this latest challenge.

I took a deep breath, mentally prepared myself for the next lapse in employment, and let the impact sink in—and immediately felt God take control. He didn't give any details, provide a timeline as to when I would get another job, or perform a cheerleading routine to pump up my spirits; He simply took control.

Matthew 26 tells the story of Judas' betrayal of Jesus. While Judas played an important part, his role was secondary. He wasn't a necessary part of God's plan concerning the ultimate sacrifice. God could have used anyone to betray the Son of Man, but He chose Judas. God could have used anyone to play the part I had been given, but He chose me. I was being reminded of this decision time and time again. God had chosen me. For whatever purpose, God decided I was the one He was going to build and reshape through these trials.

I wasn't a necessary part of the drama that began the day the plant exploded, just someone who had a role as it unfolded. God had prepared me for that event by allowing me to endure various trials, much as He had prepared Judas for betraying Jesus for thirty pieces of silver. Judas was the one who watched over the disciples' money. I was the one who watched over the inventories of finished goods and raw materials, both hazardous and nonhazardous chemicals. Judas handled the money, knew how the money was spent, and had accountability over the disciples' money. I knew what chemicals the plant had on hand, how much of each one was in stock, where each chemical was located, and other pertinent information about them. Jesus would have been betrayed even without Judas, and the plant would have exploded even without me.

A startling revelation for me was that if God wanted something to happen and I wasn't there to be a part of it, I was the one who would miss out. He would still ordain the event to happen, and if I hadn't been the one involved in the explosion, it would have been someone else, and the event would have become their testimony. Scripture tells us that even the rocks will cry out if we don't, so God has plenty of options if we decide to remove ourselves from plan A and the active role it carries and choose plan B, one of being a spectator.

Even in the midst of trials, we have an opportunity to serve. If we choose to sit back and watch, someone else will rise up and take the chance. We have to dare to be great when we are presented with an opportunity from God to be used in His service.

As I exited the building on my last day of work, Ross followed me outside. We paused for a moment by my mother's car, which I was borrowing, staring at each other and searching for something to grasp on to before moving our gazes in different directions. The breeze carried hope past me and off into the horizon as Ross began to speak.

"I'm sorry, Jason. I wish there was a way that I could hang on to you as an employee. The company is broken financially, and the directive from ownership was that we were to lay off everyone. I had plans for us to really turn this company into something dynamic. I really did."

"Ross, it's okay, really. I've been through this so many times before, it is getting to be old hat for me now. Plus, I know God will provide."

"Yes, I am sure He will."

"But since you brought it up, what kind of plans did you have for the plant?"

"Well, my intention was to have you doing the materials and production planning, working in conjunction with Gary as management. You guys were already building a strong, positive relationship, and I think we really could've blown past the ownership's expectations for growth and profitability. Plus, you and Joan have a great work relationship, too."

"Wow, Ross. That would have been great. Too bad things had to turn out the way they did. All we needed was some capital investment from ownership to make some of the equipment and processes better, and all of this mess could have been avoided. It really makes me ill that the owner couldn't see those needs as being big enough to be taken care of."

"We had that discussion several times. His response was somewhat incredulous. Even though we usually grossed $450,000 monthly, he wanted $1 million net sales in a month. He informed me that when we netted him a million bucks a month, he would get us a new building."

Shaking my head in disbelief, all I could see was that impossible amount. "A million net a month? Ross, we don't do that on average in a quarter. How in the world did he expect us to do that?"

"I don't know, Jason, I just don't know."

"Oh well, it's not like it matters now after all that's happened."

14

Taking Action

JUST LIKE THAT, MY JOB was over. It was mid-afternoon when I left the plant for the last time, so I decided to head home and take a quick nap.

As I was driving home, I noticed how much my left ankle was swelling. The swelling seemed to be increasing daily. Some days, the swelling was so severe I had to untie my shoe or remove the shoelace.

The company's workers' compensation insurance was spotty at best in communicating with the employees, and the frustrations were getting high, especially now that we had all been laid off. Harry, one of the most recent full-time hires, was ready to hire a lawyer. He began talking with other displaced employees, and the lawyer idea began gaining momentum.

Then my phone rang. "Jason, it's Harry. I guess you have heard about the lawyer idea by now."

"Yep, I am about ready to jump on board with it, especially now that the company has seen fit to lay us all off. Do you have anyone in mind?"

"Yeah, actually, I do. It is a group out of Charlotte, and we are supposed to be meeting with them in two weeks. If you want to join in with the rest of us, either let me or the lawyers know."

"Okay, I will let you know."

After hanging up the phone, I began to contemplate my options. I knew God was in control, and everything would turn out the way He had it planned. I also knew that in my few and limited conversations with the workers' compensation insurance provider, I had received no assistance regarding my injuries or concerns. My ankle continued to swell daily, flashbacks were still religiously harassing me, and my hearing had not stabilized, among other things. The workers' compensation provider had not assisted me in getting any doctors' appointments scheduled, with the exception of a precautionary hearing exam. Hiring a lawyer appeared to be a viable option to help obtain the medical services I needed.

I signed on with my coworkers two weeks later.

The lawyers went to work immediately, securing me follow-up appointments with orthopedic specialists for my ankle and ear, nose, and throat specialists for my hearing and vision. The orthopedist, Dr. Geidermann, suggested I first try physical therapy for my ankle to see if there would be any benefit.

The physical therapy was a disaster.

I began treatment at a local physical therapy office in May and continued through September. The treatments consisted of heated whirlpool baths, range-of-motion exercises, sweat, pain, tears, retelling the story of the events from the day of the explosion, and hearing the stories of other patients and their triumphs. I found out that one therapist was a cancer survivor, and as she shared her story of triumph with me, we discovered similarities in our lives that made my treatments a little more bearable.

There were days when the pain was so intense I couldn't walk when I left the physical therapy office and needed help getting to my car. There were other days when the pain was mental, and the stress of the situation added to the physical pain would overwhelm me, causing me to lose my composure and succumb to the tears.

I became depressed and found God to be the main source of strength to combat the effects of depression. Ps. 91:1–2 says, "He who dwells in the shelter of the Most High, will rest in the shadow of the Almighty. I will say of the Lord, 'He is my refuge and my fortress, my God in whom I trust'" (NIV).

These verses became a foundation for support, a reminder of the constant love, mercy, and grace that God supplies in quantities greater than we can comprehend. And He provides these every minute of every day. Yes, even when we think we are abandoned, He is there watching, waiting, patiently loving us the entire time.

There were days when the circulation and feeling in my left foot were so bad, it simply would not cooperate during the treatments. The whirlpool bath temperature would be set around ninety-five degrees, but my foot would come out looking as if it had suffered first-degree burns. There were times when my foot and my mind would battle for supremacy over which one would direct movement. My foot won most of those battles, as my mental fortitude simply was not up to the task of overcoming the lack of responsiveness. This would then create a chain reaction of events: the lack of responsiveness led to me becoming discouraged, the discouragement led to a lack of effort, the lack of effort led to prolonged soreness, and so on.

I didn't realize at the time I had a horizontal crack through the middle of my ankle bone. I just knew it hurt. There was a jagged corner of bone sharp and prominent enough to almost penetrate the skin when I turned my food inward.

The therapy eventually helped strengthen the joint and muscles in my left calf, but the pain remained. The therapists recommended that I return to the orthopedist for more tests, and an MRI was scheduled. The MRI revealed the crack, along with more tendon and ligament damage, and surgery was an option.

In October 2006, after a brief trip with my family to Charleston, South Carolina, it was time for surgery. Angie, my mother, and I got to the hospital early on the morning of surgery, and my mind and nerves went into overdrive. The flashbacks hit with the force of a tidal wave, and my system went haywire. After several trips to the bathroom and some medicine to get my nausea under control, I was able to settle down enough to prepare myself for the surgery.

The surgery was scheduled for eight that morning, but by 8:15 I was still waiting in the preparation room. Dr. Geidermann was running late, and I was informed that I would be taken back for surgery as soon as possible.

Shortly afterward, the nursing staff appeared to take me back for the surgery. I kissed Angie good-bye, told her to wait for me, squeezed her hand, and was promptly rolled down the hall. In the pre-op room, I was parked beside an older gentleman waiting on a different surgeon. We shared small talk and prayer together, and then Dr. Geidermann walked through the doors.

"Good morning, Jason. Sorry I'm late."

"It's okay. Stuff happens, right? Let's get this thing under way, though, before I get cold feet and back out." We shared a quick laugh, and Dr. Geidermann gave the signal to the operating room staff.

"If you are ready, let's go."

With that, the lights went out.

On waking up from the surgery, I felt an extra heaviness around my left leg. After pulling the covers back, I saw an apparatus around my lower left leg, beginning at my knee and reaching to my toes. Dr. Geidermann walked in the recovery room as Angie and I were examining the unit on my leg.

"I see that you are awake. Good. How are you feeling?"

"Like I just went through surgery, doc. When will it start hurting?"

"You should still feel good for a few more hours. I have written you a prescription for Percocet; make sure you take it as prescribed for pain. The soft cast you are wearing will remain on for six weeks. After that, I will see you again for a follow-up, and then you will go to a hard cast for another four weeks. At the end of the four weeks, we will take you out of the cast, give you a cane for support, and restart your physical therapy. Any questions?"

"Uh, I guess not. When am I able to go home?"

"As soon as you can stand with the aid of some crutches and are able to use the bathroom. We have to make sure all your bodily systems are functioning properly and then you are free to go."

"Okay, where's the bathroom?"

15

Recovery, Part I

At home, things started to get interesting in a hurry. The sensation returned to my foot and ankle sooner than expected, and the pain grew quickly to an almost intolerable level. Kenneth came over to my house to sit with me while Angie went into town to pick up my medicine and do a few other errands. He and I tried to pass the time by talking about football, racing, and channel surfing, but the pain continued to possess part of me. As it continued to grow in intensity, it transitioned from a pounding and throbbing pain to a burn that consumed my thoughts.

Angie returned with my pain medicine, and I promptly took some. The doses were to be taken every four to six hours around the clock, and by the second dose, the medicine was definitely working. Hallucinations mixed with the flashbacks became quite an interesting combination. There were moments when the vision of the plant exploding would manifest, and then the images would morph into various distortions of items around the house. This would continue for the next week.

I stopped taking the Percocet a week after the surgery, and the pain eventually became manageable with over-the-counter medication. I also became more mobile. My increased mobility allowed me to get outdoors and try to rehabilitate my mind. The remainder of the weeks in the soft cast passed by without incident, and finally the day arrived when I was to have the hard cast applied.

I greeted the morning of my appointment in much the same way as a child greets the morning of his birthday. I felt as if I was going to obtain a new freedom. I would be able to ditch the crutches and begin walking semi-normally by lunch.

Shortly after checking in at the doctor's office, the waiting room attendant called my name, and Angie and I were escorted to a treatment room. I handed Angie my crutches and hobbled my way to the exam table. The attendant left the room, and Angie and I waited in suspense for Dr. Geidermann.

He finally entered the room and, after the typical conversation, removed the soft cast. The sight that greeted us is forever ingrained in my mind.

As Dr. Geidermann slowly peeled away the soft cast, I saw a foot and a leg that had once been strong and were now shriveled, bruised, battered, and disfigured. I was reminded of the leper in Mark 1:40–45. I was sure the leper's condition was, at the very least, as bad as mine, but his covered most of his body. Yet he still had faith that he would be healed.

I needed to have that amount of faith. I had to remind myself that God wasn't through with me, and that He would ensure my foot, ankle, and leg were healed.

After the initial sensation of freedom returning to my foot passed, I pushed the envelope and tried to move it a few inches. The result was explosive. Pain rocketed directly from my ankle to my eyes and then into the middle of my brain. Dr. Geidermann inhaled sharply and said, "You probably shouldn't have done that just yet. It didn't cause any more physical damage, but I know it hurt."

"I don't think the word hurt does it justice," I said through clenched teeth.

After a brief discussion with Dr. Geidermann, the hard cast was applied. Connor had told me that morning he wanted me to have a blue cast, so blue it was.

Once the cast was dry and I could put weight on my foot, I was handed the standard walking boot. As anyone who has had a hard cast before can attest, those boots are proof God has a sense of humor. They are nothing more than a glorified, reverse flip-flop with extra material on the sides and two Velcro straps.

Once I was properly equipped, I was ready to attempt walking. The saying "Watch out for that first step, it's a doozy," while cliché, is very adequate for times like when I took my first step in the boot. Once again, pain shot up my leg straight to my brain. I spent four weeks in the hard cast and walking book, with each day becoming more bearable than the one before. I also grew confident that God was restoring me to a healthy state.

Though I knew God was healing the physical damage, the mental damage was still prevalent. The times when the pain would reoccur would trigger another flashback, setting my nerves on end for several hours. After a while, I would recover and push the images of destruction into the deep part of my mind where they would not be as active and annoying.

It was finally time to remove the cast. Arriving at the doctor's office, I was anxious and nervous. At last I could get rid of the cumbersome, restrictive cast stuck on my leg for the last month. However, I was unsure as to how much I could trust "that" ankle to support my weight. It had become that ankle, not my ankle. I had been so bothered by it, I had begun to disown it. I didn't claim it as part of my body; it was simply something attached to my foot and leg that caused me problems.

When the cast was removed, I was appalled at the sight. My foot was a sickly bluish purple, as if someone had melted a box of blue and purple crayons and soaked my foot in the mixture for hours. Dr. Geidermann informed Angie and me that the bruising would go away eventually, but more physical therapy was required to strengthen my leg and that ankle. My left calf had withered to almost half the size of my right calf and was obviously very unstable.

Elation over getting the cast removed turned to tempered despair at the thought of having to endure more physical therapy. My brain immediately began to fight with that ankle in the struggle for dominance. An internal conversation began to brew, gained steam, and turned into a full-fledged onslaught against my willpower. The battled raged between my determination to regain my health and the part of me that wanted to run away from the thought of therapy.

Great, more physical therapy.

Oh well, you asked for it.

I can't bear the thought of having to suffer through that junk again.

It's something that I have to do to make everything better.

If the surgery hadn't occurred in the first place, physical therapy wouldn't be necessary now.

The surgery had to happen or that ankle never would have been fixed.

So what if it wasn't fixed. Made it nine months on it while it was busted anyway.

I have to do it. End of story. I have no choice now.

Angie was looking at me, her mouth moving, but because of the intense warfare in my head, the words she was saying were unrecognizable and did not register. She gently took my hand, and at her touch, I realized I needed to dissolve the combat squads from the battlefield of my mind and tune back into the present moment.

"Are you ready to go home now?" she asked with gentleness in her voice.

"Yeah, let's go. Thanks, doc, for everything you've done."

16

Recovery, Part II

NOW THAT THE CAST WAS gone, I had a foot again. That ankle was still there, still problematic, but at last I had a foot again instead of a cumbersome club attached to my leg.

Phone calls were made, appointments were set, and I was preparing to return for more physical therapy. This time around, there was as much mental preparation as there was physical preparation. I knew what the torture would be like, having already been through it before.

Then it began—frustration, pain, discomfort, exhaustion. The cycle would repeat itself daily. For months, each day would be just as intolerable as the previous, with very little hope of the cycle being broken. Prayer was my daily supplement, my breakfast, lunch, and dinner. It was also my pillow to take a nap on, to fall asleep on, and find comfort in.

Treatment days would consist of the whirlpool bath, the bucket o' beans, resistance band exercises, and balance board work. The whirlpool bath still left my skin close to a nice strawberry color. The bucket o' beans was a plastic container filled with kidney beans and was used to facilitate the process of regaining movement in my ankle. It would remind me that I had suffered enough damage that movement was still almost impossible, and the resistance band and balance board served to demonstrate how weak that leg and ankle had become. I had been a runner in high school and to realize that my leg had lost most, if not all, of its power was a shock.

Over the months of treatment, though, my strength started to return. The circulation in my ankle and foot began improving, and with that, the prospect of whirlpool bath burns shrank. I began to see that the words God revealed to me in Jer. 29:11–13 were being made to pass. My body was slowly beginning to heal.

As the healing progressed, I realized I was running out of excuses to cover up the mental stresses I was still enduring. I began to pray about how to handle them, and God began to reveal different options for treatment. I called a psychologist and set up an appointment for a consultation.

Upon meeting the psychologist for the first time, Dr. Smith had me explain the situation. We discussed the symptoms I was having, patterns of recurrence, and other factors, and he gave a diagnosis of posttraumatic stress disorder, and borderline chronic depression. He also suggested I begin my mental rehab by taking walks along the river that runs through my town. He also suggested playing golf as another source of therapy.

Seeing as I greatly enjoyed both of those activities, I thought it was a great idea. Therapy was walking by a river and playing golf? Right up Perfect Avenue for me—until I tried it. My foot and ankle became so swollen, my next physical therapy session had to be moved up a day and doubled.

The next step in the physical therapy, intended to enable me to continue with the mental therapy that had been suggested, was to have custom-made insoles for special-order shoes. The insoles didn't work and had to be refashioned. After several attempts, the insoles were finally ready and were implemented as part of my treatment plan. However, all was not well. They size of the insole on my left foot had to be a certain thickness to properly support my ankle, but this led to pain in my hips as I was tilted at an angle when upright.

I stopped using the insoles.

My frustrations were mounting anew, and depression began its relentless siege on my mind once again. I would try to study God's word, looking for solace, comfort, anything that would help me understand why I was in this situation. When in my prayer time, a conversation with God would often go like this:

"God, I don't understand why I am in this situation. Please help me figure it out."

"You are there right now because I need you there right now."

"Okay, but when do I get to leave all this mess behind?"

Silence.

God was teaching me patience to go along with the lessons of trusting in Him that had been placed in front of me. Through the pain, tears, depression, anxiety, frustration, and more, God was slowly revealing to me how to be totally dependent on Him. There would be no more self-reliance, no more boastful self-confidence.

As I began to understand how to relax and let God handle things, another form of therapy began. My wife had been reminding me that she had a friend who was a massage therapist. This friend was very good at her craft and could possibly help me, so I gave in and allowed Angie to set up an appointment for me. My first trip to Sharon's office was only the beginning. God had orchestrated things to build my patience, begin rebuilding my body physically, and prepare me for what was to come.

When I walked into Sharon's office, I entered into a peaceful setting and knew Jesus was there with me. Sharon spoke softly; had gentle, healing hands; and was a Christian. She listened as I spoke and seemed genuinely able to connect with me. After taking a brief look at my problem areas she diagnosed my problems and we discussed treatment. The first session ended with both of us glad my wife had convinced me to come see her.

Session after session, I could feel myself healing from the inside out. Sharon worked on my back, the realignment of my spine, releasing the tension from my muscles, and getting my flexibility in my back and ankle back. Then the real work began, and God revealed why He had used my wife to get Sharon involved in my life.

After the trauma of the explosion, I did not trust anyone who wasn't part of my immediate family or one of a very select few people. I had been blown up, and my life had been turned into a chaotic mess by people I was supposed to be able to trust: my coworkers. Trust wasn't a factor even worth considering at that point in my life, but I began to trust Sharon.

Angie trusted her, and that was one of the reasons I consented to seeing Sharon to begin with.

As my treatments progressed and I could feel my body loosening up, relaxing for the first time in two years, I began to feel at ease with Sharon. We eventually began discussing the explosion and what other ways I was trying to deal with everything.

Sharon shared with me that she, too, was a major trauma survivor. She instantly gained more credibility with me at that point. I was happy to find out God had orchestrated placing me with someone who had a story similar to mine for my next phase of treatment. There is something comforting about meeting a person who has been in circumstances similar to the ones you have encountered, and I found some comfort in the knowledge that Sharon had also been there, done that.

Throughout the next several months, our friendship grew, and my body continued to heal. At the end of my visits, Sharon and I had a friendship based on Christ, and I had a better, fresher, renewed feeling about the areas of my body that had been injured.

Communication with the lawyers was heating up, as the workers' compensation portion of the case was beginning to draw to a close for each of my coworkers and me. The day of mediation arrived, and as my wife and I were making the hour and a half drive to the lawyers' office in Charlotte, we attempted to make small talk to keep our nerves at bay over the day's upcoming activities.

We arrived at the lawyers' office at nine that morning, entered a rather large conference room for a meet and greet, and then headed to separate inner offices for the mediation. The process continued forward through most of the day, and we even got to enjoy lunch that my lawyer bought (and immediately added to my bill).

Around four that afternoon, my wife and I, along with my lawyer, had agreed on an amount and that portion of the case was over. The next case was the lawsuit against the owner of the company, and it progressed similarly over the next year and a half. At the end of the year and a half, mediation similar to the one for the workers compensation lawsuit was scheduled. An amount was agreed upon, and the court date was set for the final approval by the judge.

Other surprises arrived during the time we were waiting on closure from the lawsuit. God once again blessed us (and showed His sense of humor), and on March 25, 2008, our daughter, Macey Karlton Webb, arrived a little after nine in the morning. She weighed 9 lbs 1 oz and was a carbon copy of her mother, beautiful beyond belief. Even with my history of extreme trauma, God had given us another child. God once again showed His love for us by allowing this baby to be conceived naturally, and be born in perfect health.

From the moment Macey was born, I knew she was just like her mother. As soon as I held her and began to speak softly to her, she quieted down immediately and snuggled up against my chest.

Once again, I felt my heart leave me and reach out to my daughter as it had the first time I held my son. There I stood, holding my daughter with my son waiting just down the hall to see his sister, amazed at God's graciousness. His ability to pour out love, gifts, and blessings without ceasing has always astounded me, and the first moment I held my daughter was no different.

As I watched her cry out as she became accustomed to being in this world, I spoke softly, gently, trying to calmly reassure her that everything would be okay. I knew she would face trials, problems, pain, and more in her life, but I wanted her to know that I would be there with her. I wondered how many times God had looked down at me and said the same thing, but I had just been too busy and preoccupied with myself to get out of my own way and listen to Him.

God wasn't finished handing out blessings. A few months after the birth of my daughter, He provided a new job. It was the first job I had been able to secure since the plant explosion. I obtained insurance and a steady paycheck, and we began to recoup some of the financial losses we had suffered because of the explosion. It was July 2008.

IV

2010

17

It Begins. . .Again

THE REST OF 2008 AND 2009 passed without incident. Our comfort level had begun to acclimate itself to a nice, even keel, but we were becoming complacent. Our worship was reaching new heights, and our dependence on God for sustainability was growing and so was our family. Connor was seven years old, Macey was two and a half, and both were growing quickly. The children were joining in prayer time at night, before meals, and in the mornings when we would all head our separate directions for work, school, and day care. God was growing, strengthening, and blessing our family.

Then 2010 arrived—and it began with a vengeance.

On Valentine's Day, while taking my wife out to dinner, I began a two-month battle with colitis. It's never fun to get sick, especially during inopportune moments. It's even worse when it is on date night (which is great for married couples), and especially on Valentine's Day when you're thirty miles away from home. Obviously, our date was cut short.

In March, the colitis struck again, causing bleeding when I would use the bathroom, intense abdominal cramps, and much more. I began having an internal boxing match with myself and faith in one corner, and the what-ifs in the opposite one. Rounds one and two were won by the what-ifs, but by round three, the tide had started to turn. Faith reappeared and, strengthened by the memory of the words God had revealed to me in the passage in Jeremiah, became stronger than the what-ifs.

While round three was a dead heat between the two opposing forces, round four brought the steely resolve out in the faith corner. By round five, it was a knockout: faith had prevailed.

I knew it wasn't cancer again; God had promised and delivered healing. I scheduled another doctor appointment, received treatment for hemorrhoids, and was sent home. When the medicine didn't work, I scheduled an appointment with a gastroenterologist, who in turn scheduled an appointment for a colonoscopy.

With my appointment card and prescriptions in hand, I left the doctor's office and headed to the local pharmacy. I turned in the prescriptions and called Angie. After a few minutes, the pharmacist called me to the counter and set a grocery store bag on the counter. The bag contained a box and a bottle of antibiotics—the antibiotics to help clear up the infection and the box with a much more sinister purpose.

Inside the box was a mixture I had to add water to along with a flavor packet of my choice. As the pharmacist explained—and I soon found out—it was essentially drain cleaner for my body with the taste of swamp water and chalk mixed together. (That flavor was achieved after adding the fruit-flavored packet.) I was instructed on its use and, after paying, was ready to head home.

The night before the colonoscopy passed rather eventfully, almost right until the procedure began. The swamp water and chalk flavored drain cleaner has a specific purpose – to make sure that you are as clean and empty internally as possible before the procedure. When the human drain cleaner is taken after a fast that began twenty-four hours earlier, you can be absolutely sure your body is empty of any solid food. Towards the end of the preparation treatment regimen, it feels as if you are eliminating food you haven't eaten yet, and you begin to look forward to the next mornings' procedure.

After being rolled into the procedure room, the anesthesiologist administered the first round of anesthesia. Again, I passed across the void dividing the world of the living and the realm of medically induced nothingness.

I was enjoying the best sleep I had experienced since the plant explosion when I felt myself being gently shaken. I heard my wife telling me I had to wake up, that the procedure was over and it was time to go home. I received a diagnosis of ulcerative colitis, and was handed a prescription for medicine to help the healing process.

April passed without incident, but by this point, Angie and I were constantly on edge for what could—and probably would—happen next.

18

The Storm Continues

WE TURNED THE PAGE ON the calendar and May began. The Bradford pear trees outside our house bloomed beautifully, creating a massive spread of white against a bright, clear blue sky background. The flower bed Angie and I had planted blossomed quickly, and our yard turned into a patchwork utopia, rapidly filling with color.

As soon as the flowers bloomed, it seemed as though an alarm had been set off that attracted every thunderstorm to our neighborhood. After one particularly rough, stormy Sunday morning, we returned home from church to find one of the pear trees had lost a rather large section of limbs. The damage to the house was very minor, but the yard was a mess.

I began to saw the section of tree apart to haul off and felt a sharp pinch on my elbow. I slapped the side of my arm, and the pain diminished. I continued my work, eventually removing the entire downed portion of the tree.

A few days later, I noticed a small place beginning to swell on my left elbow. As the end of May came, made an appearance, and left, my elbow had swollen so much I could not bend it, making my left arm almost useless. Here came another visit to a doctor.

The doctor on call at the urgent care office took one look at my arm and gave me two choices: "We can either open the wound site to remove the infection and toxin, or you can lose your arm." Neither of those choices appealed to me, but the losing the arm idea was non-option. So I consented to the cutting, and the "butchering" began.

Numbing my elbow was an utterly unbearable experience, with the discomfort made worse by the fact numbing medicine would have to be administered in the middle of the pocket of infection. The doctor conveniently failed to mention this before giving me the injection.

"You were bitten by a black widow spider and, in a few more days, could have quite possibly lost part of your arm," the doctor informed me as he worked. The doctor's artistry required all of fifteen minutes to carve a permanent reminder of the bite.

The procedure finished, my arm was bandaged and placed in a sling, and I was sent home. I could remove the bandages and sling a few days before our vacation began.

Once again, we encountered smooth sailing on the sea of life for a few months until Labor Day weekend. The toxins from the spider bite had not all been removed from my bloodstream and created an infection on the right side of my chest, which conveniently landed me in the hospital for a few days. IV fluids, antibiotics, and blood tests were my daily regimen for Labor Day weekend.

Three weeks later, my wife and I were making plans for a mountain getaway weekend for our wedding anniversary when the next problem arrived. On September 27, 2010, during a rainy day on the interstate, a woman decided it would be a great opportunity to have her compact car and my three-quarter-ton heavy-duty truck engage in a ballet as I was on my way home from work. The initial impact happened on the right rear corner of my truck when she lost control of her car. The result was an immediate right hand turn and head-on collision with the guardrail.

As my truck stood on its nose atop the guardrail, while wearing my seatbelt, my chest collided with the steering wheel, allowing me a direct-from-above view of the ground and the steep drop on the opposite side of the guardrail. The truck bending the guardrail acted as the force of a loaded slingshot being pulled back, and my truck became the projectile. In a blur of motion, the truck was launched backward, returning to the traffic lanes on the interstate—facing the wrong direction. I slammed back into the seat with such tremendous force that both hips, several ribs, and my left shoulder were knocked out of joint. The last image I saw was a tractor-trailer beginning to jackknife on the highway to keep from hitting me. Then the world went black.

Sometime later, which felt like three eternities but was only moments, consciousness began to grasp its fingers around my world of darkness. As the sensations of pain, numbness, and an intensely firm grip around my neck started to register with my brain, my eyes began opening. God had spared my life once again. The tractor-trailer stopped one hundred yards in front of my truck, and the driver was headed back to his cab. The woman driving the car that hit me had walked up to my truck and was screaming incoherently about the person who was driving the car in front of her. The world went black again.

One by one, the sounds of my surroundings began to register in my head, and I picked out voices.

"Sir? Hello? Sir? Are you okay?"

I tried to turn around in the seat to see what had my head pinned back.

"Don't move, sir. We are first responders who saw your wreck happen. My partner is stabilizing your neck until EMS can get here."

My eyes began darting around nervously, trying to comprehend exactly what had happened and take in the scene around me. I began trying to find my phone, as my wife and I had been talking when the accident occurred. I heard her panicked voice in the distance and finally, with assistance, got a grip on my phone. I let her know I was okay, to get someone to watch the kids, and to meet me at the hospital. Then the questioning began again from the EMTs.

"Sir, can you tell us what your name is?"

"Jason Webb."

"Where were you headed?"

"Home from work."

"Mr. Webb, we are going to help you until the paramedics can get here. Are you okay with that?"

"Yes, and thanks for your help."

I felt my phone vibrating in the middle console of my truck and had one of the EMTs answer it. It was Angie trying to find out some information and letting me know that she and Kenneth were heading to the hospital to meet me.

The world started to get fuzzy again, but just as I was about to slip across the brink of unconsciousness, I heard the ambulance pull up. The gentlemen who had been helping me began to share my personal information with the medical staff, and discussions about how to get me to the stretcher and body board were going on.

I felt the hands that had held my head and neck upright begin loosening their grip and then felt the hard neck brace click into place. The medical crew decided there wasn't enough room to get the stretcher between the truck and mangled guardrail, so one of the EMTs asked me if I was supported, did I think I could walk to the back of my truck. The question took a moment to register, and after a brief deliberation of the choices (either in my truck facing oncoming traffic or in the ambulance en route to the hospital), I decided the ambulance was the safer bet.

I assured the EMT that if I had enough support, I believed I could make it to the back of my truck and then discovered my lower left leg was pinned between the parking brake and the door. The paramedic carefully moved the brake pedal enough to release my leg. Aided by the paramedic, I slowly, painstakingly made my way to the waiting stretcher. I realized it was only eight feet or so that I had to walk, but the pain and nausea made the distance overwhelming.

After being loaded on the stretcher and wheeled into the ambulance, the pain sensors in my back really ratcheted up the torque, and my muscles began convulsing. The muscles on either side of my spine forced themselves into overdrive, tightening up with enough conviction that my brain quickly gave up trying to control them. This act of mental submission allowed the pain-o-meter to crack the upper limit of what I could bear, and everything started to go dark. I fought against the surging current of black and forced myself to see images of Jesus and my family to stay conscious during the ride to the hospital.

During the battle against the waves of darkness that threatened to overtake me, the EMT with me asked questions about the wreck, my family, and my faith—anything to keep me alert and talking. It was during this conversation that I overheard her ask the driver if we were headed the right way. That question, followed by his response of "I'm not sure," was enough to shatter the intensity of the moment. We all began laughing, each laugh causing more pain in my back.

Finally, the ambulance arrived at the hospital, and the flurry of movements began anew. The EMTs were blurs in their uniforms, handing me off to the hospital staff with a good-bye and reassurance that their prayers would be with me and I was in good hands.

A doctor appeared outside my door and instructed the nurse to give me a shot of morphine for the pain and then get my intake information. *Intake information? What are they talking about? How I am taking the morphine? In a shot I guess.*

Before the nurse could get into the room to administer the morphine, the state trooper who was reporting on the accident appeared in front of me. He had followed the ambulance to the hospital to find out my condition.

"Mr. Webb, I just wanted to check on your condition and let you know I had your truck towed to a local garage. I already have the facts from the lady who was driving the car that hit you, so I don't need to question you about the accident. Here's my cell number on the accident report and a card of the company that towed your truck. Please call me if you need anything else."

My wife, her face streaked with tears, arrived with Kenneth. He was the first to speak.

"Well, bro, you did it again. When are you gonna learn your lesson?"

"I don't know, man. I just got bored and decided to see if the truck would jump the guardrail I guess."

The nurse came in and gave me the shot of morphine to help quell some of the pain.

"Honey, where are you hurting at?" Again, Angie was asking what she could do to help fix the problem, and I could tell from the look in her eyes she was hurting almost as much as I was.

Moments later, the X-ray tech, Ray, appeared and let me know it was time for more tests. He was excellent at his job. He sympathized with my pain and did his best to accommodate my condition.

As Ray wheeled me back to radiology, we made small talk through the pain, which resounded through my body with each bump of the hospital bed. The X-rays were quite a challenge, with Ray needing me to position myself in ways that were not possible at the moment. Twenty three X-rays later, Ray placed me in a wheelchair for the return trip and rolled me back to my room.

The doctor returned a brief time later with the report stating there was nothing broken, but several joints had been dislocated, and I had a full column spinal bruise, a major case of whiplash, and lots of soft tissue damage. I would be sore, requiring pain medication, and would need to follow up with my doctor in a few days.

As Angie and I let out a collective sigh of relief, the doctor handed us my discharge papers, and Angie and Ken helped me walk to the van.

We rode by the garage where my truck had been towed before heading up the interstate to go home. During the ride, Angie and Ken didn't ask many questions about what had happened to cause the accident; instead we passed the time comparing my life to the experiences found in the book of Job. The trials that Job endured seemed like the foundation of my previous few years. Once again, the resolve appeared and took my mind captive. If Job could persevere through his trials and still remain faithful to God, so could I.

A few days later, I saw a lawyer to assist me with my bills and the insurance company of the woman who had caused the accident. The lawyer immediately set me up with a chiropractor since I was barely walking. The office staff began making phone calls to help me schedule doctor visits and other treatments as necessary, and I was on my way to recovery.

The initial visit to the chiropractor was quite the experience. As the two chiropractors, Dr. Toskey and Dr. John began my workup, small talk began. When asked about my medical history, I recounted all the wonderful experiences God had led me through. Dr. Toskey eventually said, "This is the worst case of whiplash and spinal column bruising I have ever seen in my thirty-two years of practice." Wow. What a reassurance.

My new routine consisted of acupuncture (despite my fear of needles) and the stretching and readjusting of my spine, hips, neck, and chest combined with soft tissue therapy work. Eventually, after months of treatment, I achieved the maximum medical improvement of about eighty-five percent of my original mobility and was released from medical care by both doctors.

The accident had caused my posttraumatic stress disorder to return, and it did so with evil intentions. The fact that it had been repressed for some time had served no other purpose than to let it build up pressure, waiting to be released by some new event. In a fashion similar to a two-liter soft drink bottle being shaken violently right before the cap is removed, the posttraumatic stress exploded when the accident removed the cap I had placed over it.

My sleepless nights returned, and my temper was short. My nerves were frayed, especially when making the commute from home to work and back again. I found myself driving different routes to avoid going past the accident site and trying to change the times I would allow myself to be on the road.

I finally succumbed to Angie's persistent urgings and found another psychologist who specialized in severe trauma cases. Months passed during which the therapy, along with constant prayer, began to make changes. I could feel the stress and chains of worry being removed as I allowed myself to open up and listen again to what God was telling me. I found a way to allow myself to let go and let God take care of it all—again. I was recovering, finding peace in Jesus, and beginning to trust enough to remember the promise God had revealed to me when He led me to Jer. 29:11–13 in the waiting room before my cancer treatments began.

V

BLIND FAITH, A CUP OF COFFEE, AND JESUS

19

Reflections

MORNINGS ARE ONE OF MY favorite times of the day. I especially love autumn mornings when the brisk air causes you to catch your breath. The fog that appears as I exhale a deep breath serves as a reminder of the pot of coffee brewing in the kitchen.

I start my day by remembering everything God has brought me through, the promises He has made and not broken but exceeded and the reassurance that I am His and He is mine. That deal was secured by the sacrifice made by Jesus on the cross.

As I sit down to enjoy a cup of coffee, I like to invite Jesus to enjoy one with me. It gives us time to talk, which usually starts off with me expeditiously running through prayers, concerns, and more, and always ends with Jesus speaking or moving, and my heart, mind, and emotions being stilled.

A pot of coffee is almost always good for either a conversation between those near the pot or a time of reflection. Both of these activities inevitably find their way into my coffee time. I like reflective, stainless steel coffee pots. When you look at them, you can see your own reflection. I wonder if that is the same appearance God sees when He looks at me. It is like looking in a mirror. Where we see our imperfect skin, a spot we missed shaving, or other "flaw," we tend to focus our attention there. When God looks at us, though, He sees everything we see but more. We mean more to Him than we can comprehend, and He looks into our heart as He looks at us. When we smile, He smiles. When we cry, He gives us a shoulder and a tissue. When we hurt, He comforts. He sees one of His children who meant enough to Him for the ultimate sacrifice to be ordained, orchestrated, and accomplished.

I open up my day with a "Good morning, God, thanks for another day" and then greet my wife and kids. During my personal quiet time, I often reflect on the people God has allowed to become part of my life. There have been seasons where certain people would arrive, be part of my life, and then move on. Ecclesiastes 3 tells us there is a time for everything. Everything has its own season—friendships, acquaintances, ministries, jobs. Some seasons may be longer than others, but the main emphasis is to grasp the blessings and opportunities God provides for us during that season and allow ourselves to be used by Him.

We will see our faith manifest when we allow ourselves to be molded during that particular season. Of all the seasons shared in the earlier chapters of this book, God taught me a different lesson during each of them. Patience and trust in Him were the constant themes He tried to get me to understand, but He also showed me compassion, love, and a deeper, more intimate faith. He taught me how to grow relationships, how to strengthen them, and how to walk away from them.

Forgiveness. One word, one meaning, yet we are so easily confused on this topic. Trust. Again, one word, yet something we aren't very good at. Listening. Wow. There's a strong conflict of interest for us. Searching, seeking, asking, and waiting. These are also characteristics we probably wouldn't include in our list of strongest assets.

As I sit back now with my pot of coffee and the opportunities to reflect on everything God has brought me through over the years, I see how His hand was guiding each of my steps. I see how He orchestrated the events in my life to teach me forgiveness, trust, and how to listen. I begin to understand how God kept reminding me about patience, and how to allow Him to have total control over all of my life.

I see how my faith has grown, and I have witnessed how God has used my testimony to impact the lives of other people struggling with similar situations. As the coffee pot empties cup by cup, I realize that God has poured Himself into my life in a way not so different from how I fill my cup. God pours a little more of who He is into our lives at different times, allowing us the opportunity to consume what He graciously gives without overwhelming us.

20

Forgiveness

Why is forgiveness so hard? Why is it so difficult for us to say to someone "I forgive you"? As imperfect people with an internal perfection complex, we seem to be able to say, "They should forgive them of _____ (insert action here)" or, better yet, "If I was in their shoes, I could forgive (someone's name)."

When the rubber meets the road, do you actually forgive? I know I don't always follow through with that course of action. I will consider it, but I don't always allow myself to do it. That, admittedly, is one of my numerous shortcomings.

We are taught in Matt. 18:22 to forgive. Not just once but a multitude of times. Exactly how many times must we forgive? Not just seven but seventy times seven for each transgression against us. That's a lot of forgiveness.

Are we actually capable of forgiving someone four hundred and ninety times for each thing we feel he or she has done against us? Probably not, but I feel the point Jesus wants us to understand is that we are not to hold a grudge against the guilty party. If we were to be held accountable for everything we have ever done against someone, much less what we have done that grieves God, the weight of our sin would be so great it would crush us.

Matt. 6:9–15 gives us another set of scripture that elaborates on forgiveness: "This, then, is how you should pray: Our Father, in heaven, hallowed be your name, your kingdom come, your will be done on earth as it is in heaven. Give us today our daily bread. Forgive us our debts, as we also have forgiven our debtors. And lead us not into temptation, But deliver us from the evil one. For if you forgive men when they sin against you, your heavenly Father will also forgive you. But if you do not forgive men their sins, your Father will not forgive your sins" (NIV).

That prayer lays the ground rules for forgiveness: forgive and you will be forgiven; don't forgive and you will not receive forgiveness. Biblical examples abound through the life of Christ concerning forgiveness.

Let's look at the last supper Christ shared with the disciples. It was a time of fellowship, forgiveness, and mystique. I can envision the scene the disciples observed as they entered the chamber where Jesus had them gather for the meal.

They walk in and there sits their friend and teacher, brother, the Son of God. He looks at them with a compassionate, loving smile and greets them warmly. He invites them to take a seat as He gives each person a hug. One by one, as they sit down, the disciples notice a bowl of water on the floor next to where Jesus is seated.

The whispers begin: "I wonder why there is a bowl of water to wash our feet. Who is going to do it? Not me. I hope He doesn't ask me to do it. I mean, I will wash His feet, but Peter's? No way. I mean, have you seen Peter's feet?"

I feel sure Jesus sat there with the same loving smile, a broken heart full of forgiveness, and laughed on the inside. His thoughts may have been, "Oh, you confused, selfish people whom I love so much. I am going to completely surprise you when I sit down to wash everyone's feet. Peter is going to want more though. He has always been a compulsive person. Moderation has not been his strongpoint, but that is one reason I will build my church on him."

I am sure the scene was full of confusion, spoken and silent, as Jesus stood up, laid his clothes to the side, and wrapped a towel around his waist. The custom of the day was that someone who was a servant of the household would wash the travelers' feet. But here was Jesus preparing to do just that.

Keep in mind that people didn't wear tennis shoes and socks, the roads weren't paved, and they lived in a dry, dirty climate. With all those factors, you can begin to imagine just how dirty and grimy everyone's feet were. Yet Jesus, the Son of God, washed the disciples' feet.

He also did this as an act of forgiveness and love. He knew Peter would deny Him three times that night. He knew Judas would betray Him. He knew the disciples would run and hide once He was arrested. He knew Thomas would doubt after the resurrection. But yet He still loved them enough to wash their feet and forgive them ahead of time.

He knows before we do when we are about to sin, and He stands ready to forgive us. All we have to do is ask. He still loves us through it. Jesus' love is without end, strong enough to weather any storm.

Have you ever paid attention to what forgiveness can actually do for a person? It allows healing. It opens the door for restoration. It can restore friendships and families. It also strengthens the bonds of family, friendships, work relationships, and marriages. How many times in our marriage do we know we either need to forgive or be forgiven, but we are mired in self-pity, allowing stubborn pride to reign supreme for the moment? When we succumb to stubbornness and prideful actions, we allow the moment when forgiveness would have the greatest impact to fly by and leave us suffocating in a missed opportunity.

I have seen many situations where husbands will buy flowers or take their wife out on an expensive date as an apology. I have found, however, that while those are nice gestures and my wife appreciates them, she really wants to hear a heartfelt "I'm sorry." And the same is true for women who need to apologize to their husbands. That simple two-word statement will open the door to forgiveness, and restore and heal any injury a relationship has suffered.

We see forgiveness exemplified in the book of Jonah. God told Jonah that he should go to Nineveh to preach, but Jonah declined the opportunity to serve and ran. We all know how the story goes after that: God sent a storm, Jonah was thrown overboard from the boat on which he was sailing, the storm ceased, and a whale swallowed Jonah. An interesting thing here is that God forgave Jonah, delivered him at the shore of Nineveh (courtesy of the whale), and allowed him a second chance to serve and minister.

God wasn't done yet, though. As Jonah delivered the word God had given him, the people of Nineveh began to repent and seek God. Once again, God forgave. When Jonah got upset at God, and the situation as a whole, he let his selfish desires get the best of him. He got in the way of what God was doing, and let his goals take priority over what God had determined would happen. But God still forgave Jonah.

How many times have we been like Jonah? We ask, seek, and fervently pray for something, then when it doesn't work out the way we want it to, we throw a temper tantrum. "God, it's not fair! I did what your word tells me to! Why didn't it happen like I was asking you for? What else could I have done to have helped it happen?"

When my work exploded, I threw temper tantrums. I prayed and prayed, seeking answers as to why I had to deal with everything that was going on, yet, none of it was my fault. I wanted answers to questions that I was afraid to ask. Why did it happen? Why do I have this diagnosis of posttraumatic stress disorder and borderline chronic depression? I became angry, and wanted answers. I demanded answers, stomped my feet, shouted at God about how unfair it was, and held onto this anger. In the midst of my loud, exorbitant exclamations of what I felt was right, I began to hear a faint whisper telling me I was still loved. I finally allowed God to begin the process of healing in my life.

It is in our nature to be selfish and to want more than we really need. Do you remember that infamous line our parents used to tell us when we were children? "Looks like someone's eyes are bigger than their stomach." We are disappointed, aggravated, and sometimes even angry with God when things don't go the way we feel they should. Yet He forgives us. He still loves us, and there isn't anything we can do about it.

21

Blessings

WHEN WE THINK OF BLESSINGS, what comes to mind? A financial windfall? Good health? Good weather on a vacation? Many things can be labeled as blessings in our daily life. However, it is up to us to recognize the gifts from God, both large and small, for what they truly are—blessings.

As you have read through this book, you have experienced the trials on which my testimony has been built. James 1:2-4 says this concerning trials and blessings: "Consider it pure joy, my brothers, whenever you face trials of many kinds, because you know that the testing of your faith develops perseverance. Perseverance must finish its work so that you may be mature and complete, not lacking anything"(NIV).

How can a trial be a blessing? God will allow your situation to get as rough as possible and then turn it into a blessing to reveal His power, love, and mercy to you. He will use obstacles in your life to bring out a deeper level of faith in you that you had not been able to enjoy previously.

Have you ever noticed trees on a mountainside? The old, weather-scarred trees are the ones that stand the tallest in the forest, aren't they? These are the trees that have stood the test of time—blistering summer heat, freezing winter temperatures, wind, rain, and other weather events. Yet they persevere and grow stronger and taller through the onslaught.

We must allow God to mold us as the trees have been. We must sink our proverbial roots deep into the soil of His word and be willing to stand through the trials that come our way. As a result, we are blessed with more experience and a stronger knowledge of and deeper relationship with Christ. As we grow stronger in our relationship with Jesus, we dive deeper into Him, and our foundation becomes stronger. The trees on the mountainside don't give when storms arise; they don't fall apart as the storms rage around them. They are firmly rooted in their foundation.

When we allow ourselves the freedom to turn to Christ and seek Him first, our foundation is strengthened. Then, as the storms in our life rage around us, we may be swayed and knocked around a bit, but the blessing we receive is that our foundation does not crumble. We find the strength to go forward and continue on thanks to our relationship with Jesus. What a blessing to receive!

When you think about blessing someone else, what typically is the first thing you think of? Giving him money? Maybe a ride when he is having car trouble? Praying for him? What about something as simple as a sincere smile and a question about how his day is going? Sometimes, something as simple as asking how someone's day is going will brighten his or her outlook on life.

A prayer partner of mine, Mike, and I frequently go to lunch together. During these lunch outings, we have experienced some very intense moments with God. One particular day, we decided to go to a certain restaurant, and as soon as we pulled into a parking spot, a man approached us. This man, Ray, was homeless, broke, and trying to collect aluminum cans to take to a local recycler to turn in for money. Ray approached us and asked for a dollar to get a cup of coffee. Mike and I immediately offered to take him to lunch.

The five dollars we spent on a meal for him wound up opening a door for God to send us a blessing. Throughout the course of conversation, we found out that Ray had been a carpenter and roofer and had worked in construction for many years. Sickness had hit his family, then divorce, then financial troubles, and as a result, he wound up homeless. The closest family he had was thirty miles away, and he managed to eat between one and two complete meals a week. Circumstances that were beyond his control had pushed him into his current living situation, and he had become desperate for anything to hold onto as a source of hope.

As we began sharing the gospel of Jesus Christ with him, we noticed a change starting to overtake him. His eyes became wet with tears, and he poured out his heart to us. He had accepted Jesus at a previous time in his life but had fallen out of touch with Him due to all the events of the past several years. Ray made a comment with a huge impact: "You guys have helped me remember how to smile."

He had not smiled in such a long time, it was a foreign concept to him. The joy of life, especially life in Jesus, had escaped his grasp. God revealed something to all three of us that day. No matter what our circumstances, He will send who He needs to be present at the absolute perfect time. Yes, Mike and I bought lunch for Ray and gave him a small financial gift to help, but God revealed things to us that still stick with us today.

We can find joy in helping others. It is a joy that goes deeper than a smile from seeing someone enjoy a blessing. It transcends the immediate reaction of "Oh, isn't that great? I am so glad that I was able to help them." It reaches the depths of your heart when you realize what you have been blessed with and how much for which you have to be thankful.

When Ray told us that day that he had found a reason to smile again, Jesus smiled down on all three of us. Christ had used Mike and me as a means to bring a spark of happiness and joy back into Ray's life, and what a blessing it was for us!

Another prayer partner and friend of mine, Victor, has a testimony that will grab you and shake you, and God uses it for a youth ministry in the greater San Diego area. His story is one of deliverance from a lifestyle of drugs, gang violence, alcohol, and more. The way God broke these chains in Victor's life, and how he has used his story in ministry represents the completely life altering power of the grace of God.

In other ministries I have been involved in, there have been countless opportunities to share with people the hope that is found in Jesus. No matter what the situation is, we as Christians are called to share that blessing with others. When you look back over your life, you inevitably see instances where you have received blessings. Remember how those blessings impacted your life? Imagine the impact you could make on someone's life when you bless them!

Jer. 29:11–14 tells us God has a special plan to bless us:

For I know the plans I have for you, declares the Lord, plans to prosper you and not to harm you, plans to give you hope and a future. Then you will call upon me and come and pray to me, and I will listen to you. You will seek me and find me when you seek me with all your heart. I will be found by you, declares the Lord, and will bring you back from captivity. I will gather you from all the nations and places where I have banished you, declares the Lord, and will bring you back to the place from which I carried you into exile. (NIV)

What a promise we have to stand on in those verses straight from the heart of God! He has blessings stored, waiting on us to seek Him first. Matt. 6:33 tells us, "But seek first his kingdom and his righteousness, and all these things will be given to you as well."(NIV) We have to search for God's will in our life, above anything else, and then as our faith grows, our relationship with God matures and takes precedence in our lives. As the percentage of our life that is given to God increases, we will begin to notice things as blessings that we may have attributed to coincidences, chances, or accidents.

As Jer. 29:14 says, we find God when we seek Him with all our heart. Our selfish nature sees things our heart longs for as things that we want, when we want them, doesn't it? As we start to explore and dive deeper into the relationship between our heart and God's plan, we will begin to uncover more and more blessings in our lives. We will see our lives becoming enriched in ways only God could create, strengthen, and sustain!

22

People

HAVE YOU EVER NOTICED HOW some people show up for a certain amount of time, stay through a rough spot, and then are gone? Sometimes, people you meet will become lasting friends who stay with you through thick and thin, good times and bad. They will climb the mountains with you, trudge through the valleys, and swim down the river of life with you. Some people will appear for a season and walk out of your life as quickly as they walked in it.

If you are old enough, take a moment and think back to the people you hung out with in school. Who were your high school friends? What about your college crew? Are you still close with any of those people? Which group do they fit into: friends for a season or friends for life?

I have had opportunities to meet numerous individuals through several ministries of which I have been a part that have challenged me, helped me grow, taught me, and blessed me. A band I was in played at a youth worship event several years ago, and I shared my cancer testimony with the youth group. As the ministry time was ending, a young lady approached my band members and me with tears streaming down her face. Through her tears, she shared a part of her life that she had been able to give to Jesus that night. Her mother had succumbed to cancer years earlier, when this young woman was four years old, and she had been holding onto that pain for the last ten years. Through the message

God delivered that night, she was finally able to let go of the torment of losing her mom. I may never see that young lady again, but I know God worked on her that night and took those chains of bondage from her heart through my ministry.

Some people are put in our life to teach and guide us, while others we meet are in our life to learn from us. Elijah had a strong relationship with God, but the day came when he was to be an example for someone else. Enter Elisha.

Elisha walked with Elijah, learning constantly. In the book of Exodus, Joshua followed Moses at all times, learning every minute of the day. In both situations, the students were being taught and instructed to accomplish more of what God had planned for them.

In Acts 16:6–10, we see where someone else joins Paul on his journey. Luke, who was a doctor, wrote the book of Acts. Paul meets Luke in Troas, and the pronouns used in the book change at that point. Previously, the pronouns had been "they," "he," and "him." At this point, Luke becomes an active part of the book, and the wording changes to reflect him. Words like "we" and "us" replace they, he, and him.

Like Paul accepted Luke into his inner circle, we must realize when God is sending someone to us so he or she may become part of our inner circle. We have to make sure that the people we let into that inner circle are those who share our beliefs and values. Luke became part of the group that Paul used to bounce ideas off of, the prayer circle that he asked to pray for confirmation for God's will.

Think about the people you have allowed into your life. Have they become part of your trusted inner circle, or are they people you associate with? Who spends time daily praying for you, and is your spiritual covering? To whom do you turn when you need prayerful advice on something? Who holds you accountable in your walk with Christ? If you don't have anyone who fits that description, prayerfully seek someone out. Ask God to send someone who will keep you constantly covered in prayer.

Mike and I find ourselves praying for each other frequently. As we seek answers for each other through prayer, I often find Mike praying and asking God to send me one of the blessings God has appointed for Mike if it is in His will and would help provide an answer. I pray in the same accord for Mike when he is in need of an answer. For whom do you pray in a similar fashion? Who prays for you that way?

From the beginning of time, God created us to need each other. He established the first family in Genesis when He created Adam and Eve. Our need for community has not diminished. We all still experience that need each day; it is up to us to discern through prayer how to fulfill that need in our lives.

We must also be aware of the effects we can have on other people. Imagine being able to stop an ice cream truck and buy ice cream for a group of young children. As the group is enjoying their ice cream, you notice another child standing at the end of the block, grinding the toe of his shoe into the asphalt and wishing he was part of the group.

At that moment, you have a choice: include the child who is separate from the group or don't. What are the ramifications of these choices? You can choose to invite the child over and buy him some ice cream, thus enabling him to become part of the group. However, you also can pretend not to notice his saddened state and exclude him, possibly reinforcing the feeling of being an outcast.

Granted, with children, it seems to be a fairly obvious answer, but what about adults who come to church seeking answers, support, help, or friendship? We have all seen the disheveled person who comes seeking, knocking, and looking for God. We all have been the one who said, "I wonder why that person is here," most likely with a scowl on our face. The thought crossed our mind, causing us to wonder why that person felt entitled to stain the carpets in our church with his problems. Is that the type of person you want to be? Or will you allow yourself the freedom in Christ to share that person's pain and the love of Christ?

The woman whose husband has broken the sacred bond of marriage, the elderly gentleman whose wife has just passed, the family who just lost a parent—sometimes all these people are looking for is someone to remind them that Jesus values them, loves them, and cares about what they are going through. A kind word, a smile, or sharing Ps. 91:2 with someone can remind him that the Creator of the universe loves him enough to know he is hurting and help him through that hurt. Allow God to work through you to help these people get their ice cream.

23

Exalt!

THE CONCEPT OF PRAISE AND worship appears in the Bible in a plethora of instances. It is used in times of great exuberance, joy, blessings, festivities, and worship. It also is used in circumstances of pain, suffering, loss, confusion, temptation, and trials. Apparently, there is something to praise and worship, don't you agree? We see examples of people throughout the Bible worshipping during the tough times, setting a precedent for us to follow.

Exodus 32–33 sets an example for us to follow when we are faced with difficult circumstances. Moses had been spending time in the presence of God at the top of Mount Sinai while the Israelites were left in the valley. God informed Moses that the people were losing their focus on Him and beginning to seek out other things to replace God in their worship. Moses pled for the people and headed back for the valley, carrying the tablets on which God had written.

When Moses approached the valley, he entered into a situation that tested his temper, self-restraint, and more. He saw the Israelites dancing around a golden calf, singing and worshipping it. In a fit of rage, he threw the tablets down, breaking them into pieces. After getting the people back in order, Moses returned to the mountaintop to meet with God again.

Aren't we the same way? Don't we have a tendency to lose control of ourselves when things aren't how we think they should be? What about when they aren't how we want them to be? Don't those moments seem to happen when we find ourselves like Moses, coming down from the mountaintop after being with God?

When we feel that we are spiritually on a mountaintop, we are opening ourselves up to be tested. We let our guard down because our comfort level is high. We get complacent because things are going our way. Oftentimes, we experience events that build our faith only to slide down the mountain, return to the valley, and have it tested. Usually, we fail miserably. I know I do. I would be willing to bet most of you have as well. Take a moment and honestly examine yourself and see where you fit in.

We find it easier to praise and worship God when things are good. That is exactly what we should do. However, we need to remember to praise God and thank Him through our actions and speech during the tough times. This is the basis for James 1:2. When we show joy in the midst of our trials, our faith in Jesus will display itself through our speech, actions, and reactions to the situation. As we focus more on our joy found in Christ, our trials become more bearable and less of a strain. We are able to find God in the heart of our crisis, and our focus on Him becomes more evident to those around us.

Matt. 8:23–27 tells us when Jesus and the disciples were on the Sea of Galilee. The disciples faced a storm of overwhelming proportions, and in the face of seemingly insurmountable odds, lost sight of their faith in Christ and His promises.

As they were sailing on the sea, a major storm blew in and began to sink the boat. Afraid for their lives, the disciples looked at Jesus, wondering why He wasn't joining with them in using buckets to bail out the water. They spotted Him peacefully sleeping in a corner of the boat as if the storm was no real concern to Him.

When the disciples woke Him, He paid no attention to the storm at first. Instead, He rebuked the disciples. Jesus asked them, "You of little faith, why are you so afraid?" (NIV). Then he calmed the storm and raging sea. Jesus had already told the disciples they were going to opposite shore, but instead of trusting in the word of God, they allowed themselves to fall back into the flesh and allow perception to override truth. Don't we often find ourselves following the same path? Most of the time, people tend to react like water: we find the easiest course of action and take it. More often than not, that easier course of action is not to trust where God is leading us.

Do we let ourselves get in the way of where God is leading us? Aren't we each control freaks in our own way? I am guilty as charged. I try daily to release control of my life to God, seeking where He is going to lead me and trying to learn how to walk down the path He has set before me. It is not always the easiest path, but scripture tells us the path is narrow and the travelers are few. We can't maintain control of our life and expect God to lead us where He needs us to be. How can we allow ourselves to open up for His will to become manifested in us when we have our own agendas? We can't.

To experience everything God intends for us and grow into the disciple He has planned for us to become, we have to release our inhibitions and relinquish control of our life. We have to become bold enough in the strength we find in Christ to step out of our comfort zone and separate ourselves from the world's ideologies that keep us from the love and will of God. As Paul writes in Rom. 12:2, we cannot conform to the patterns of this world because we are set apart from them by the blood of the Lamb. We are consecrated by a holy and pure sacrifice, one that was orchestrated by the Creator of the universe so that we may draw closer to Him.

As we exalt the matchless name of Jesus, whether in an organized worship service; in a secluded, private moment of communion; or during any other part of our day, we allow ourselves to draw closer to God. We open our heart and life to the Father of all creation, accepting His offer of an all-encompassing package, including grace, love, mercy, wisdom, and peace. As we become the disciples in the boat, waking Jesus up in the moment of our fear, we will begin to realize that He is ever present, offering this package at all times, and it is up to us to accept the offer.

24

Coffee, Cake, and Ice Cream

As I sit and enjoy my cup of coffee, I thank God for the blessings He has provided. The simple joys in life, like the peacefulness on a brisk morning while enjoying that cup of coffee and the chance to watch my family, are blessings. Each prayer we share together, each song we sing, each opportunity to worship we share are all blessings from God. Hearing each of my children sincerely spend time in prayer before everyone leaves for the day, before meals, and nightly displays the influence God has in their lives.

I enjoy being able to sit down in my favorite chair with a bowl of ice cream, a piece of cake, or both for a few moments of reflection on the day. Inevitably, those moments become better as Connor and Macey realize that I have ice cream and make a hurried dash to my lap to politely and conveniently eat it for me.

As those moments occur, Angie and I look at each other and laugh, enjoying the closeness of our family. While I watch the kids devour the cake or ice cream, I reflect on the joy I experience while they are in my lap, spending time being close with me. I imagine God experiences the same joy when, in our excitement, we rush to share a special dessert with Him and spend time in His lap. Even though the dessert is the reason why Connor and Macey come rushing to me, the quality time we spend together always lasts longer than the food.

The moment we run to God to spend time with Him is the moment our relationship grows stronger. The love He has for us far surpasses anything we can fathom and, like me with my family, He wants to spend that special time with us.

The next time you and your family are together with that pot of coffee, piece of cake, or bowl of ice cream, enjoy the moment. Remember that God longs for those moments with you as well, and allow yourself the opportunity to crawl into His lap for special time with Him. He is our Father, and He loves us more than we could possibly know.

CPSIA information can be obtained
at www.ICGtesting.com
Printed in the USA
LVOW11s2234271116

514692LV00001B/180/P

9 781449 750558